O God of earth and altar,
   Bow down and hear our cry;
Our earthly rulers falter,
   Our people drift and die;
The walls of gold entomb us,
   The swords of scorn divide;
Take not Thy thunder from us,
   But take away our pride.

From all that terror teaches,
   From lies of tongue and pen;
From all the easy speeches
   That comfort cruel men;
From sale and profanation
   Of honor and the sword;
From sleep and from damnation,
   Deliver us, good Lord!

Tie in a living tether
   The prince and priest and thrall;
Bind all our lives together,
   Smite us and save us all;
In ire and exultation
   Aflame with faith, and free,
Lift up a living nation,
   A single sword to Thee.

G. K. Chesterton

Earth & Altar

The Community of Prayer in a Self-Bound Society

Eugene H. Peterson

INTERVARSITY PRESS
DOWNERS GROVE, ILLINOIS 60515

InterVarsity Press is the book-publishing division of Inter-Varsity Christian Fellowship, a student movement active on campus at hundreds of universities, colleges and schools of nursing. For information about local and regional activities, write IVCF, 233 Langdon St., Madison, WI 53703.

Distributed in Canada through InterVarsity Press, 860 Denison St., Unit 3, Markham, Ontario L3R 4H1, Canada.

Cover photo: Gary Irving

ISBN 0-87784-334-1

Printed in the United States of America

Library of Congress Cataloging in Publication Data

Peterson, Eugene H., 1932-
   Earth & altar.

   Includes bibliographical references.
      1. Prayer.   2. Bible.   O.T.   Psalms—Criticism,
interpretation, etc.   3.   United States—Moral conditions.
I.   Title.   II.   Title: Earth and altar.
BV210.2.P48   1985   248.3'2   85-5261
ISBN 0-87784-334-1

17	16	15	14	13	12	11	10	9	8	7	6	5	4	3	2	1
99	98	97	96	95	94	93	92	91	90	89	88	87	86	85		

For Constance Fitzgerald, O.C.D.

Preface

This is a book about changing the life of America, from the inside out. The change is already in process. Many are involved in it. I hope to enlist others in the action. The source action is prayer.

I have written a book for Christians who want to do something about what is wrong with America and want to plunge into the center, not tinker at the edge. I have chosen eleven psalms that shaped the politics of Israel and can shape the politics of America, and I have taken them seriously in the way that they were intended to be taken seriously, as prayers that shape national life. I have written to encourage Christians to pray them both as children of God with eternal destinies and as American citizens with daily responsibilities in caring for our nation.

But writing about prayer is not prayer; neither is reading about it. Prayer is, well—prayer. I wish it were easier than it is. And I wish that I could provide a formula that would more quickly attract spectators into the action. But I can suggest a procedure.

1. Gather a few friends and commit yourselves to meet together eleven times for the "unselfing of America."

2. Meet regularly for periods of one and a half hours *Begin* the time by praying the psalm in unison. *Then* spend thirty to forty minutes reading and discussing what I have written in reflection on the psalm-prayer. *Next,* pray the psalm a second time, again in unison. *Follow* that unison prayer with fifteen minutes of attentive, disciplined silence, letting the prayer settle into your inward parts, being a company of obedient believers before the Lord. *End* the silence by a unison praying of the psalm for a third time.

3. Observe the ways in which God draws you into further acts of obedience in the more public parts of your life. Don't be in a hurry for this. Don't assume that it will be with your prayer partners or only with Christians. Don't suppose that you have to come up with your own program. Be ready to be drawn into actions beyond or different from your accustomed routines. See what happens.

4. Meet with your friends for a final time, one year after your initial meeting (schedule this meeting at your eleventh session). Talk with one another about what has been going on: What unselfing are you aware of that you are engaged in? What connections have been made in your life between earth and altar? Who else has been part of the connecting work? What continuing "unselfing of America" has God drawn you into? What in this can you trace to the source action of prayer? This is a meeting to share out of your own life and to observe in the lives of your friends your deepened participation in what God is doing in the world.

1 The Unselfing of America

Why do the nations conspire,
  and the peoples plot in vain?
The kings of the earth set themselves,
  and the rulers take counsel together,
  against the LORD and his anointed, saying,
"Let us burst their bonds asunder,
  and cast their cords from us."

He who sits in the heavens laughs;
  the LORD has them in derision.
Then he will speak to them in his wrath,
  and terrify them in his fury, saying,
"I have set my king
  on Zion, my holy hill."

I will tell of the decree of the LORD:
  He said to me, "You are my son,
  today I have begotten you.
Ask of me, and I will make the nations your heritage,
  and the ends of the earth your possession.
You shall break them with a rod of iron,
  and dash them in pieces like a potter's vessel."

Now therefore, O kings, be wise;
  be warned, O rulers of the earth.

Serve the LORD with fear,
  with trembling kiss his feet,
lest he be angry, and you perish in the way;
  for his wrath is quickly kindled.

Blessed are all who take refuge in him.

Psalm 2

My experience and observations have taught me to
recognize in this degeneration into the All-Self the
opponent of mankind, steadily increasing in might during
the epochs of history, but especially in our time. It is none
other than the spirit itself, cut off, that commits the sin
against the holy spirit.

Martin Buber[1]

On the "ribbon of highway" that stretches "from California to the New York island"—the great American Main Street—the mass of people seem completely self-absorbed. One hundred and fifty years ago Alexis de Tocqueville visited America from France and wrote: "Each citizen is habitually engaged in the contemplation of a very puny object, namely himself."[2] In a century and a half things have not improved. For all the diverse and attractive, buzzing and mysterious reality that is everywhere evident, no one and no thing interrupt people more than momentarily from obsessive preoccupation with themselves.

America is in conspicuous need of unselfing. Concerned observers using the diagnostic disciplines of psychology, sociology, economics and theology lay the blame for the deterioration of our public life and the disintegration of our personal lives at the door of the self: we have a self problem and that problem is responsible for everything else that is going wrong.

A few people carry Ban-the-Bomb placards to try to wake up the masses to the danger in which a century of mindless selfishness has delivered us. Desperately they try to avert the destruction of the earth by protesting the insanities of militarism, greedy and reckless practices that ravage our streams and forests and air, and bloated consumerism that leaves much of the world hungry and poor. Others hand out Repent-or-Perish tracts in an attempt to startle the shuffling crowds into dealing with their souls, not just their selves. They urgently call attention to the eternal value of the soul, present the authoritative words of Scripture that tell us who we are and what we were made for, and ask the big question, "Are you saved?" Both groups attract occasional flurries of attention, but not for long. The two groups, while they both care, don't seem to care much for each other. If they talk to each other at all, it is in contempt. One group wants to save society, the other to save souls, but they recognize no common ground. From time to time other solutions are offered: psychologists propose a therapy, educators install a new curriculum, economists plan legislation, sociologists imagine new models for community. Think tanks hum. Ideas proliferate. Some of them get tried. Nothing seems to work for very long.

In Alexander Solzhenitsyn's extensively reported and now famous sermon to America, delivered in 1978 at Harvard University, he said, "We have placed too much hope in politics and social reforms, only to find out that we were being deprived of our most precious possession: our spiritual life. It is trampled by the party mob in the East, by the commercial one in the West." We are, he thundered, at a "harsh spiritual crisis and a political impasse. All the celebrated technological achievements of progress, including the conquest of outer space, do not redeem the 20th century's moral poverty." We need a "spiritual blaze."[3]

What the journalists did not report—not a single pundit so much as mentioned it—is that a significant number of people are actually doing something about Solzhenitsyn's concern. I work with some of these people, encouraging and sometimes providing guidance. Thousands of pastor, priest and lay colleagues are similarly engaged. They are doing far more for both society and the soul, tending and fueling the "spiritual blaze," than anything that is being reported in the newspapers. The work is prayer.

Prayer, of course, has to do with God. God is both initiator and recipient of this underreported but extensively pursued activity. But prayer also has to do with much else: war and government, poverty and sentimentality, politics and economics, work and marriage. Everything, in fact. The striking diagnostic consensus of modern experts that we have a self problem is matched by an equally striking consensus among our wise ancestors on a strategy for action: the only way to get out of the cramped world of the ego and into the large world of God without denying or suppressing or mutilating the ego is through prayer. The only way to escape from self-annihilating and society-destroying egotism and into self-enhancing community is through prayer. Only in prayer can we escape the distortions and constrictions of the self and enter the truth and expansiveness of God. We find there, to our surprise, both self and society whole and blessed. It is the old business of losing your life to save it; and the life that is saved is not only your own, but everyone else's as well.

The Source Action

Prayer is political action. Prayer is social energy. Prayer is public good. Far more of our nation's life is shaped by prayer than is formed by legislation. That we have not collapsed into anarchy is due more to prayer than to the police. Prayer is a sustained and intricate act of patriotism in the largest sense of that word—far more precise and loving and pre-serving than any patriotism served up in slogans. That society continues to be livable and that hope continues to be resurgent are attributable to prayer far more than to business prosperity or a flourishing of the arts. The single most important action contributing to whatever health and strength there is in our land is prayer. Not the only thing, of course, for God uses all things to effect his sovereign will, and the "all things" most certainly includes police and artists, senators and professors, therapists and steelworkers. But prayer is, all the same, the source action.

The single most widespread American misunderstanding of prayer is that it is private. Strictly and biblically speaking, there is no private prayer. *Private* in its root meaning refers to theft. It is stealing. When we privatize prayer we embezzle the common currency that belongs to all. When we engage in prayer without any desire for or awareness of the comprehensive, inclusive life of the kingdom that is "at hand" in both space and time, we impoverish the social reality that God is bringing to completion.

Solitude in prayer is not privacy. The differences between privacy and solitude are profound. Privacy is our attempt to insulate the self from interference; solitude leaves the company of others for a time in order to listen to them more deeply, be aware of them, serve them. Privacy is getting away from others so that I don't have to be bothered with them; solitude is getting away from the crowd so that I can be instructed by the still, small voice of God, who is enthroned on the praises of the multitudes. Private prayers are selfish and thin; prayer in solitude enrolls in a multivoiced, century-layered community: with angels and archangels in all the company of heaven we sing, "Holy, Holy, Holy, Lord God Almighty."

We can no more have a private prayer than we can have a private language. A private language is impossible. Every word spoken carries with it a long history of development in complex communities of experience. All speech is relational, making a community of speakers and listeners. So too is prayer. Prayer is language used in the vast contextual awareness that God speaks and listens. We are involved, whether we will it or not, in a community of the Word— spoken and read, understood and obeyed (or misunderstood and disobeyed). We can do this in solitude, but we cannot do it in private. It involves an Other and others.

The self is only *it*self, healthy and whole, when it is in relationship, and that relationship is always dual, with God and with other human beings. Relationship implies mutuality, give and take, listening and responding. "I wonder," wrote Baron Friedrich von Hügel to his niece when she was learning to pray, "whether you realize a deep, great fact? That souls—all human souls—are deeply interconnected.

That we can not only pray for each other, but *suffer* for each other? Nothing is more real than this interconnection—this gracious power put by God into the very heart of our infirmities."[4] If the self exploits other selves, whether God or neighbor, subordinating them to its compulsions, it becomes pinched and twisted. If the self abdicates creativity and interaction with other selves, whether God or neighbor, it becomes flaccid and bloated. So neither by taking charge nor by letting others take charge is the self itself, but by being in relationship. How do we develop that? How do we overcome our piratical rapaciousness on the one hand and our parasitic sloth on the other? How do we develop not only as Christians but as citizens? How else but in prayer? Many things—ideas, persons, projects, plans, books, committees—help and assist, but the "one thing needful" is prayer.

The School of Prayer
The best school for prayer continues to be the Psalms. It also turns out to be an immersion in politics. The people in the Psalms who teach us to pray were remarkably well integrated in these matters. No people have valued and cultivated the sense of the person so well. At the same time no people have had a richer understanding of themselves as a "nation under God." Prayer was their characteristic society-shaping and soul-nurturing act. They prayed when they were together and they prayed when they were alone, and it was the same prayer in either setting. These prayers, the psalms, are terrifically personal; they are at the same time ardently political.

The word *politics*, in common usage, means "what politicians do" in matters of government and public affairs. The word often carries undertones of displeasure and disapproval because the field offers wide scope for the use of power over others, which power is often abused. Politics is smudged with greasy adjectives: ruthless, corrupt, ambitious, power-hungry, unscrupulous. But the word cannot be abandoned just because it is dirtied. It derives from the Greek word *polis* ("city"). It represents everything that people do as they live with some intention in community, as they work toward some common purpose, as they carry out responsibilities for the way society develops. Biblically, it is the setting in which God's work with everything and everyone comes to completion (Rev 21). He began his work with a couple in a garden; he completes it with vast multitudes in a city.

For Christians, "political" acquires extensive biblical associations and dimensions. So rather than look for another word untainted by corruption and evil, it is important to use it just as it is so that by it we are trained to see God in the places that seem intransigent to grace. The people who warn that "religion and politics don't mix" certainly know what they are talking about. The mix has resulted in no end of ills—crusades, inquisitions, witch hunts, exploitation. All the same, God says, "Mix them." But be very careful how you mix them. The only safe way is in prayer. It is both unbiblical and unreal to divide life into the activities of religion and politics, or into the realms of sacred and profane. But how do we get them together without putting one into the unscrupulous hands of the other, politics *using* religion or religion *using* politics, when what we want is a true mixture, politics *becoming* religious and religion *becoming* political? Prayer is the only means that is adequate for the great end of getting these polarities in dynamic relation. The psalms are our most extensive source documents showing prayer in action.

The Psalms are an edited book. One hundred and fifty prayers are collected and arranged to guide and shape our responses to God accurately, deeply and comprehensively. Everything that it is possible to feel and experience in relation to God's creative and redeeming word in us—John Calvin called the psalms "an anatomy of all the parts of the soul"[5]—is voiced in these prayers. Two psalms are carefully set as an introduction: Psalm 1 is a laser concentration on the person; Psalm 2 is a wide-angle lens on politics. God deals with us personally, but at the same time he has public ways that intersect the lives of nations, rulers, kings and governments. The two psalms are together by design, a *bi*nocular introduction to the life of prayer, an initiation into the responses that we make to the word of God personally ("blessed is the *man*," 1:1) and politically ("blessed are *all*," 2:11).

Psalm 1 presents the person who delights in meditating on the law of God; Psalm 2 presents the government that God uses to deal with the conspiratorial plots of peoples against his rule. All the psalms that follow range between these introductory poles, evidence that there can be no division in the life of faith between the personal and the public, between self and society. Contemporary American life, though, shows great gulfs at just these junctures, and at least one reason is that we love Psalm 1 and ignore Psalm 2. Christians at prayer reunite what everyone seems hell-bent and habitually to put asunder. Because prayers like Psalm 2 are so neglected in America right now, it has seemed to me strategically important to reintroduce several as source prayers for the "unselfing of America." These psalms are the material evidence and forms of prayer that have been in partial eclipse. Praying them, or after their manner, breaks through the barrier of the ego and into the kingdom that Christ is establishing.

We often imagine, wrongly, that the psalms are private compositions prayed by a shepherd, traveler or fugitive. Close study shows that all of them are corporate: all were prayed by and in the community. If they were composed in solitude, they were prayed in the congregation; if they originated in the congregation, they were continued in solitude. But there were not two kinds of prayer, public and private. It goes against the whole spirit of the psalms to take these communal laments, these congregational praises, these corporate intercessions and use them as cozy formulas for private solace.

God does not save us so that we can cultivate private ecstasies. He does not save us so that we can be guaranteed a reservation in a heavenly mansion. We are made citizens in a kingdom, that is, a society. He teaches us the language of the kingdom by providing the psalms, which turn out to be as concerned with rough-and-tumble politics as they are with quiet waters of piety. So why do we easily imagine God tenderly watching over a falling sparrow but boggle at believing that he is present in the hugger-mugger of smoke-filled rooms?

In a time when our sense of nation and community is distorted, when so many Christians have reduced prayer to a private act and when so many others bandy it about in political slogans, it is essential that we recover the kingdom dimensions of prayer. For many, recovery begins in attending to the ancient and widespread work of unselfing that is evident in the psalms. It will gain momentum as fresh prayers are offered to the "God of earth and altar," whom G. K. Chesterton petitioned with great passion as our century opened.[6]

Assembled and Dispersed

This unselfing is taking place all across the land. Bands of people meet together regularly to engage in the work. Disbanded, they continue what they began in common. They are persistent, determined, effective. "The truly real," Karl Jaspers noted, "takes place almost unnoticed, and is, to begin with, lonely and dispersed. . . . Those among our young people who, thirty years hence, will do the things that matter, are, in all probability, now quietly biding their time; and yet, unseen by others, they are already establishing their existences by means of an unrestricted spiritual discipline."[7]

Assembled in acts of worship, they pray. Dispersed, they infiltrate homes, shops, factories, offices, athletic fields, town halls, courts, prisons, streets, playgrounds and shopping malls, where they also pray. Much of the population, profoundly ignorant of the forces that hold their lives together, does not even know that these people exist.

These people who pray know what most around them either don't know or choose to ignore: centering life in the insatiable demands of the ego is the sure path to doom. They affirm Wendell Berry's judgment: "If we are to correct our abuses of each other and of our land, and if our effort to correct these abuses is to be more than a political fad that will in the long run be only another form of abuse, then we are going to have to go far beyond public protest and political action. We are going to have to rebuild the substance and the integrity of better minds, better friendships, better marriages, better communities."[8] They know that life confined to the self is a prison, a joy-killing, neurosis-producing, disease-fomenting prison. Out of a sheer sense of survival they are committed to a way of life that is unselfed, both personally and nationally. They are, in the words of their Master, "light" and "leaven." Light is silent and leaven is invisible. Their presence is unobtrusive, but these lives are God's way of illuminating and preserving civilization. Their prayers counter the strong disintegrative forces in American life.

We don't need a new movement to save America. The old movement is holding its own and making its way very well. The idea that extraordinary times justify extraordinary measures is false and destructive counsel. We don't need a new campaign, a new consciousness-raising, a new program, new legislation, new politics or a new reformation. The people who meet in worship and offer themselves in acts of prayer are doing what needs to be done. They welcome others to join them. Their acts of prayer are not restricted to

what they do on their knees or at worship. Even as the
pray-ers move into society, they move us into society. There
is no accounting for exactly where we end up: some are
highly visible in political movements while others work
obscurely and unnoticed in unlikely places.[9] We learn to be
obedient to what the Spirit is doing in us and not to envy or
criticize those whose obedience carries them down different
paths. Sometimes what others do looks like disobedience;
sometimes they appear to abandon the passion for prayer in
the passion for action. But the faithful who continue at
prayer enfold the others and sustain them in the petition,
"Deliver us from evil."

These citizens have unmasked the devil's deception that
prayer is a devotional exercise in which pious people engage
when they are cultivating some private felicity with the
Almighty or to which profane people are reduced in
desperate circumstances, but that for people in the so-called
real world the way to get things done is by committee, by
machine or by a public relations campaign. They have
recognized the deep, embracing, reforming, revolutionizing
character of prayer: it is essential work in shaping society and
in forming the soul. It necessarily involves the individual, but
it never begins with the individual and it never ends with the
individual. We are born into community, we are sustained in
community; our words and actions, our being and becoming,
either diminish or enhance the community, just as the community either diminishes or enhances us.

Prayer acts on the principle of the fulcrum, the small point
where great leverage is exercised—awareness and intensification, expansion and deepening at the conjunction of
heaven and earth, God and neighbor, self and society. Prayer
is the action that integrates the inside and the outside of life,
that correlates the personal and the public, and that
addresses individual needs and national interest. No other
thing that we do is as simultaneously beneficial to society and

to the soul as the act of prayer.

The motives of those who pray are both personal and public, ranging from heaven to earth and back again. They pray out of self-preservation, having been told on good authority that only the one who loses his life will save it. They also pray as an act of patriotism, knowing that life is so delicately interdependent that every act of pollution, each miscarriage of justice, any capricious cruelty—even when occurring halfway across the country or halfway around the globe—diminishes the person who is not immediately hurt as much as the person who is. This *insight* is not specifically Christian; the pagan Marcus Aurelius, for instance, saw it plainly: "All things are interwoven each with the other: the tie is sacred, and nothing, or next to nothing is alien to ought else."[10] But the *strategy* is Christian.

Prayer is a repair and a healing of the interconnections. It drives to the source of the divisions between the holy and the world—the ungodded self—and pursues healing to its end, settling for nothing less than the promised new heaven and new earth. "Our citizenship is in heaven," say those who pray, and they are ardent in pursuing the prizes of that place. But this passion for the unseen in no way detracts from their involvement in daily affairs: working well and playing fair, signing petitions and paying taxes, rebuking the wicked and encouraging the righteous, getting wet in the rain and smelling the flowers. Theirs is a tremendous, kaleidoscopic assemblage of bits and pieces of touched, smelled, seen and tasted reality that is received and offered in acts of prayer. They obey the dominical command, "Render to Caesar the things that are Caesar's and to God the things that are God's."

2 Unself-Made

On the holy mount stands the city he founded;
  the LORD loves the gates of Zion
  more than all the dwelling places of Jacob.
Glorious things are spoken of you,
  O city of God.

Among those who know me I mention Rahab and Babylon;
  behold, Philistia and Tyre, with Ethiopia—
  "This one was born there," they say.
And of Zion it shall be said,
  "This one and that one were born in her";
  for the Most High himself will establish her.
The LORD records as he registers the peoples,
  "This one was born there."

Singers and dancers alike say,
  "All my springs are in you."

Psalm 87

**The one who is born again cannot be scrupulously and
anxiously preoccupied with himself, although he lives in this
experience. His life has become new because, being
oriented towards the new creation, he lives in the presence
of the Spirit and under his influence, the "earnest of glory."**

Jürgen Moltmann[1]

We were barely out of the driveway and on our way home to Maryland when we got the question, "What's 'mating'?" The highlight of our vacation visit with friends in a Chicago suburb had been the birth of a litter of kittens. Our seven-year-old daughter was totally captured by the messy, marvelous miracle of birth. She watched. She exclaimed. She asked questions. The older children teased her with half-answers. When she pressed for more they told her condescendingly that she would have to ask her parents.

"What's 'mating'?" My wife and I knew that this question would be put to us at some point and had talked over the best ways to respond. We had planned that we would direct a childish curiosity about sex into an awed and respectful appreciation for life. But neither of us had expected the question this soon, so our exact reply was still unformulated. Driving through Chicago traffic requires concentration, so I was forced to let my wife ad lib what we had always agreed would be a joint response. We want to be at our best for such occasions, fresh from rehearsal with our notes in hand, but we never are. We are caught napping.

Is it possible to avoid reducing the answer to a few angular facts or blurring it in a mist of euphemism? No words seem adequate for telling the glory. Still, *something* has to be said and in words that will direct a seven-year-old not only to facts but to truth. The conversation spurted and faltered, took wrong turns, made cumbersome detours. For the next several hours the intricate, lifelong process of sex education moved from the nonverbal to the verbal. It was a memorable time: electric with curiosity, intense with caring. It had surprising shifts from clumsiness to eloquence, epiphanies of insight, stretches of puzzled silence.

The Wonder of Birth

Psalm 87 is an exclamatory, stuttering, excited response to birth. Birth is announced three times: "This one was born there" (v. 4); "This one and that one were born in her" (v. 5); "This one was born there" (v. 6). Birth. Birth. Birth.

Scholars who like sentences neat and orderly complain that this is the most mangled and disordered text in the Psalms.[2] The sentences are incomplete. Connective words are omitted. Transitions are abrupt. Images appear distorted. But poets (and parents) know that ambiguity is unavoidable in the big questions, at the great passages. They not only tolerate, they actually cultivate ambiguity. They know that to make things clearer and more orderly than they are experienced is to misinform. The disordered text of Psalm 87 is not, I think, the consequence of sentences that were lost or dislocated in the centuries of copying and transmission. Far more likely, it is honest, awkwardly spontaneous prayer in the presence of an excess of meaning, a surplus of reality.

Birth. How does it happen? What makes it happen? As common as it is, it never loses its power to catch our attention, move us to wonder, rouse our curiosity. Why is there something rather than nothing? How does life suddenly present itself out of the darkness, in the midst of pain? With all the crying, why the joy? Should we not mourn, knowing that the child is born to trouble just as sparks fly upward? Sure of the hurt and rejection and sorrow that await this infant, would not hand wringing be the appropriate response? Some, it is true, prevent birth. Some abort births. But most do not. The overwhelming, instinctive consensus of the human race is that life is good. Every birth is a fresh, pure invasion of life into our death-compromised living. Despite the pain of childbirth, the enormous amount of work required in rearing an infant to adulthood and the uncertainties of disease and accident, birth is good news.

Still, despite the frequency of birth and our irrepressible

delight in birth, we commonly and quickly drift away from attending to its meaning. Exuberance over a marvelous life shades into dread of a certain death. We are surprised out of our socks by this vigorous life but before long are hemmed in by all the signs of destruction. Then, set in the presence of birth again, we are caught up in mystery. We respond with awe. Why? We can explain the process of birth. We know all the physiological and genetic details. But none of our explanations accounts for the awe.

Parents do not sit down with chromosomal blueprints to plan a baby, working out hair color, skin texture and body type. It would be absurd to pretend to program a specific stature, a particular IQ and the vocational aptitude that will equip the child for the best paying profession in twenty-five years. When we enter the reproductive process, we do not calculate statistical probabilities in cool detachment. We do not meticulously check off one by one the staggering sum of physiological details that converge in conception and birth. We are ushered into a mystery that overwhelms us. Our intentions play a part but in no way the largest part.

In the early years of this century there was a great deal of enthusiasm for eugenics. The program was to preselect potential parents by the same principles that have bred better sheep and goats. At the time there was a celebrated exchange between the brilliant but ugly George Bernard Shaw and a dazzlingly beautiful but empty-headed actress from the London stage. She gushed, "Oh, Mr. Shaw, we really ought to have a child, don't you think? What a prodigy the infant would be with my looks and your brains!" Shaw replied, "But what if it got my looks and your brains?"

No. In the presence of birth we do not calculate, we marvel. We exclaim, "This one was born there . . . this one and that one were born in her . . . this one was born there." In the presence of birth we are at the source of life. Our preoccupations with survival and our forebodings of death

recede for a while. Spontaneity breaks through. For a few
moments, at least, we are out of ourselves. Martin Buber
wrote, "Because each man is unique, another first man
enters the world whenever a child is born. By being alive,
everyone groping like a child back to the origin of his own
self, we may experience the fact that there is an origin, that
there is creation."[3] The most ordinary birth is far more than
we can achieve by our best efforts and highly sophisticated
technology. Here is mystery, but a mystery of light not
darkness, full of goodness, brimming with blessing. Every
birth powerfully recalls us to this source: we have our origins
in someone other than ourselves, and greater than ourselves.

Nations, Not Babies
Five births are named in this psalm:
> *Among those who know me I mention Rahab and Babylon;*
>> *behold, Philistia and Tyre, with Ethiopia—*
> *"This one was born there," they say.*

What is going on here? These are the names not of persons
but of nations. The imagination does a backflip: we thought
we were paying attention to cooing and crying babies; we are
in fact confronted with fierce and frightening nations. These
are Israel's enemies: Rahab (an ancient name for Egypt), the
nation that had cruelly enslaved Israel for over four hundred
years; Babylon, who had knocked down the Jerusalem walls,
plundered the temple and taken the people into a devastat-
ing exile; Philistia, the implacable, marauding, coastal enemy
with a well-deserved reputation for brutal insensitivity to all
moral and spiritual realities; Tyre, rich and worldly merchants, the robber barons of the ancient world, whose luxury
had degenerated into decadence; Ethiopia, soldiers from the
sub-Sahara who hired themselves out as mercenaries. How
did these five ancient foes get to be included in a prayerful
reflection on the marvels and mysteries of birth? There is
only one satisfactory answer, incredible as it sounds: They

got there by being born again.

All over the world, the most unlikely people were finding new life in God, new life that can only adequately be described by the radical, life-radiating metaphor of birth. This transnational, transcultural, transracial phenomenon is one of the unlikely but happy results of the scattering of the Hebrew people by persecution and exile into the surrounding nations. The people among whom they were dispersed watched them, observed their way of life, looked over their shoulders as they read and copied their Scriptures, asked them questions about their faith and their God.

The Hebrews were not an aggressively proselytizing people, but they were an intensely serious people—serious about the meaning of life, serious about covenant with God. They did not campaign to convert others to their way of life, but their faith was contagious. The peoples among whom they lived were attracted by the dazzling intensities of their worship and were drawn into the maturing pilgrimage of holiness.[4] They left their superstitions. They left their games with spirits and divinities. They left their dull preoccupations with the self. They discovered, through the witness of the Jew, the reality of God who created, who entered into suffering, who carved out a way of redemption. They believed. They became Jews. It was a marvelously attractive life: separation from the ways of the world, concentration on the ways of God. It never became a mass movement, but nothing rivaled it for intensity, creativity and influence.

Every year, Jews who were able came back to Jerusalem to celebrate the great turning points of their faith: Passover, Pentecost, Booths. Strange people began showing up in the pilgrim bands, people with the wrong shade of skin, the wrong shape of nose. No one familiar with Hebrew experience could have anticipated this. The Jew was used to being an outsider in the world of culture, a stranger and an alien. The faith of Israel had never been a popular religion, even in Israel itself where it was constantly upstaged by Baalism, which catered to the appetite of the crowds. It made no appeal to what the majority of people thought that they wanted in a religion. The Jew was always a minority and often a persecuted and suffering minority.

The appeal was authenticity: a living God and a passionate people. In every nation in which Jews were living, searching people perceived in the speech and song and prayers of these Jews a revelation of a holy God and evidence of healthy humanity. They were drawn to these Jews, joined them, entered the way of faith. Before long they also were making pilgrimages to Jerusalem. Over the decades and centuries, the people who streamed across the roads of the Middle East looked less and less like Jewish tribes and more and more like the United Nations. A person standing on the Jerusalem city wall and watching that procession approach might well say, combining the awe and surprise with which we greet a newborn infant with the curiosity and pleasure with which we identify out-of-state license plates,

> *Among those who know me I mention Rahab and Babylon;*
>   *behold, Philistia and Tyre, with Ethiopia—*
> *"This one was born there," they say.*

Born again. Born in the faith that draws them to worship in Jerusalem. Born in the faith preached on the feast days. Then this person watching the parade turns and sees the international assemblage of people inside the city gates and exclaims over the city itself,

> *And of Zion it shall be said,*
>   *"This one and that one were born in her!"*

Mother Zion: Jerusalem important not as a political capital or as a cultural mecca, but as a *birth* place.[5] Personal wholeness comes into being here, out of Zion's womb. An unlikely family has been thrust into the world from this matrix: who could have guessed that Egypt, Babylon, Philistia, Tyre and Ethiopia would acknowledge a common parent? Zion's womb, the place of revelation and worship and, finally, of incarnation. We enter the realm of transformation and we leave transformed.

Several hundred years later, Jesus drew from the psalm the phrase that focused his extraordinary late-night conversation with Nicodemus, "You must be born anew." Nicodemus and Jesus both prayed the Psalms. It was the prayer book in which they had both been reared. How many times had Nicodemus said or sung,

The LORD records as he registers the peoples,
   "This one was born there."

But, as often happens with the familiar, the psalm was exterior to him, a pious legacy out of the past. He was never "in" the prayer. Now, talking with Jesus, he was.

Physical birth is one marvel, spiritual birth is another. The one is quite as incredible as the other. In contemplating either or both we reach our source: we find that we are not self-made but God-made.

The City of God
Significantly, the city is the site for these exclamations on birth.

On the holy mount stands the city he founded;
   the LORD loves the gates of Zion
   more than all the dwelling places of Jacob.
Glorious things are spoken of you,
   O city of God.

We must ponder God's love of the city, for there has been a great split in Christian consciousness between our personal identity as people of faith and our political responsibility as citizens in the nations. We delight in new birth but become jaded with adult life. Our best instincts rise to the surface as we hold and cuddle the newborn; we are not at all endeared to the foul-smelling drunk who sits down beside us on a crowded bus, even though the actual inconvenience to us of the baby far exceeds that of the derelict. We love to welcome converts but grumble mightily about the government that we live under, both in the nation and in the church. There are vast areas in the Christian community where all sense of citizenship has been lost and only the identity of new birth retained. But there is no trace of this split in biblical experience.

The newborn of Psalm 87 do not run away from the city to pursue God in private, they stream into it where they become participants in its government. As an act of prayer, the personal (one's birth) is combined with the public (the city). Infants grow up to be citizens. The life that is celebrated in the infant develops into responsibility exercised by the citizen.

It is the city, not the country, that the newborn enter. In the country we might manage a life on our own and indulge in fantasies of being self-made. At least there we need not rub shoulders with people who are not congenial to us nor depend on the services of people who complicate our lives. But not in the city. The city involves us in city affairs, in politics. We are thrust, whether we like it or not, into transportation patterns, business transactions, workings of a judicial system and much more. Moreover, we are faced with acting responsibly in the midst of it.[6]

The city of God of which "glorious things are spoken" is not, of course, just the Jerusalem that rival politicians argue over and journalists report on, but neither is it dematerialized. It is the city as God is working his purposes in it and as God's glory radiates from it, but an actual city all the same, a city of church and culture, of worship and weather. The city is referred to twice by the personal pronoun *her* (v. 5), a mother who gives birth to an international progeny. But those references are enclosed by the geographical pronoun *there* (vv. 4, 6). A granite mountain is under it; hinged gates open into it. *There.*

Spiritual birth lands us in a physical city. We find ourselves not only as brothers and sisters in a family but as citizens in a metropolis (literally, "mother-city"). We not only have our names registered on the birth rolls but also on the tax rolls, which means that we take on responsibilities for the common good. Praying Psalm 87 develops our conscious commitment to the public good and helps us to see the world of politics as biblical, not alien, ground.

Mother Zion
On my first visit to Jerusalem, I arrived in the late afternoon. I wanted to get to the Western Wall by sundown, the beginning of Sabbath. It was late. I did not know my way. I ran through the narrow, crowded streets of Jerusalem asking for directions. After several wrong turns and out of breath, I was there. The Wall. A few stones in the lower part of the Wall are all that remain of the biblical temple complex. There is a paved court area in front of the Wall where people gather for prayer. For Jews the Wall is the holiest place on earth.

Most holy places are architectural splendors: Gothic cathedrals, Hindu temples, Buddhist shrines, Muslim mosques. There is nothing splendid about this wall. Those who come there face a featureless expanse of stone. Those who pray there stand exposed to the elements. No beauty radiates from it. No drama develops out of it. But we do not ask for beauty or entertainment in a mother. We simply want to be at the source. Mother Zion. The place of birth. That and that alone accounts for the "glorious things" spoken of her. The simple but immense fact of motherhood subordinates all other considerations.

Then it was sundown. The signal was given. Sabbath began. I stood before the plain, unprepossessing Wall, deeply moved by a torrential convergence of memories. I was standing where David ruled, where Solomon built, where Isaiah preached, where Jeremiah wept. The place where

Jesus taught and suffered, died and was raised. I became
aware of chanting in the distance, behind me. I turned and
saw about three hundred young men (rabbinic students from
the Yeshiva, I learned later) seven abreast, arms linked
across shoulders, singing as they moved in a rhythmic and
joyful solemnity across the plaza toward the Wall. When they
arrived in the courtyard before the Wall they formed a large
circle, singing and dancing at the place of prayer.

It was one of the most emotional moments of my life. Deep
feelings of surprising intensity surged within me. The holy
place (the Wall), the holy day (the Sabbath), the holy city
(Jerusalem). And the throngs of holy people—every race
visible, numerous languages audible. It all came into physical
and vocal expression for me in the dancing and chanting
young men. The final sentence of Psalm 87 was suddenly in
my mind as an epigram to the moment,

Singers and dancers alike say,
    "All my springs are in you."

Song and dance are the result of an excess of energy. When
we are normal we talk, when we are dying we whisper, but
when there is more in us than we can contain we sing. When
we are healthy we walk, when we are decrepit we shuffle, but
when we are beyond ourselves with vitality we dance.

Where do we get the energy that lets us live beyond
ourselves, unself-made, singing and dancing? *In you*—the
place of worship, the place of preaching, the place of prayer,
the place of politics. The place that God established for
revelation and rule. The place that affirms the invisible in
our visibilities, the time and place set apart to attend to what
is going on around us, beneath us—and now in us. *In you*—
where things get started, the place of wellsprings, the deep
unstoppable source of new life pushing up through strata of
sin and indifference and stupidity and then bursting into
fountains of song and dance. Praise somersaults. Obedience
cartwheels. "I skip a grace rope to a Christ tune."[7]

3 Unself-Centered

The LORD says to my lord:
  "Sit at my right hand,
till I make your enemies your footstool."

The LORD sends forth from Zion
  your mighty scepter.
    Rule in the midst of your foes!
Your people will offer themselves freely
  on the day you lead your host
  upon the holy mountains.
From the womb of the morning
  like dew your youth will come to you.
The LORD has sworn
  and will not change his mind,
"You are a priest for ever
  after the order of Melchizedek."

The Lord is at your right hand;
  he will shatter kings on the day of his wrath.
He will execute judgment among the nations,
  filling them with corpses;
he will shatter chiefs
  over the wide earth.
He will drink from the brook by the way;
  therefore he will lift up his head.

Psalm 110

In the Biblical world of thought man is not expected to be centered upon his own personality, but on God. . . . Their interest was in a divine drama, not in a human personality; in supernatural happenings, not in the charm of a gracious Galilean.

Donald Baillie[1]

Things are not going very well these days. As a matter of fact, they never have. It is most odd. We live in the midst of extravagant beauties. The earth beneath us and the heavens above us contain shapes and sounds and colors that take our breath away. We ourselves are a marvel of staggering proportions: there is no end to the exuberance of poems, photographs, stories, landscapes, portraits, concerts, machines, tools, buildings, gardens, bridges, engines, dams, lyrics, sonnets, mosaics, sculpture, pottery and fabrics that human beings make. The American government has been, many people think, the most successful combination of political freedom and responsibility that the world has yet seen. Given the wildly beautiful and awesome land that is our home, the high intelligence and marvelous sensibility of men and women, and the conspicuous success of our political experiment in democracy, why are things so lousy? Why don't things work better? After all these centuries of lectures and sermons, symphonies and legislation, revolutions and railroads, why aren't we all scholars and saints? Thomas Hardy's epitaph is curt and cynical: "After two thousand years of Christian mass / We've got as far as poison gas."[2]

Is there anything to do about it? Most people think that there is. True, there are days when it looks as if the race is between bigotry and apathy, between the people who blame all our ills on a hated enemy and the people who have succumbed to the nothing-can-be-done disease. But in fact an enormous amount of energy is poured out each day to make things better: care for the environment, compassion for the hurt, concern for the poor, diligence in government. Great armies of people are out there teaching, healing, legislating, guiding, comforting, rehabilitating. Evil in both its obvious and subtle forms is being fought.

But the impressive number of people committed to doing something about what is wrong with the world does not always bolster hope. A close observation of the lives of those who are trying to do something about the mess around us and an unsentimental look at the results of their efforts are not always heartening. Why, for instance, do people who do good so often behave so badly? Doing good brings out the worst in some people. Why do they become so bad-tempered, so abrasive, so self-righteous? Why do so many impressively launched crusades run out of gas so quickly? Why do so many vigorous moral causes have such short lives? Why does so much well-intentioned, righteous fervor dribble out into sentimentalism? Plunging into the battle does not always bring the intended results. Sometimes our efforts make things worse. Sometimes they make us worse.

Recentering Prayer
Christians wake up in the middle of this mess every day and get out of bed to do something about it. What do we do? If we polled our colleagues, as every now and then someone does, we would get a bewildering variety of responses. One of the responses, though, that would be in predictably short supply would be "pray." I don't mean that our polls would show that Christians do not pray but that most do not see prayer as the central and essential action to remedy the mess that we are in. Prayer is understood rather as a private, "in-house" activity. When it does occur in the public sector, it is ceremonial.

This understanding and practice of prayer is so common and accepted among us that it comes as a shock to learn that Christians in other times and places have taken a decidedly different position. The difference is clear in what we know of the Christian community in the first century. That era, in contrast to ours, was regrettably deficient in matters of poll taking and statistical analysis, so we lack the kind of evidence that we are used to having provided for us. But we do have the New Testament and find that the most popular psalm in it is the 110th—quoted seven times and alluded to fifteen times.[3] No other psalm comes close. The community of first-century Christians pondered, discussed, memorized and meditated on Psalm 110. When they opened their prayer book, the Psalms, the prayer that they were drawn to and that shaped their common life was Psalm 110. What twentieth-century American has so much as heard of Psalm 110?

The informal polls that I have been taking for a number of years show that the American favorite is the 23rd, which is not even quoted once in the New Testament. By contrasting our preference with that of the early Christians I do not intend anything invidious. Psalm 23 deserves its popularity. It has brought and continues to bring a true word of God and develops a deep, authentic relationship with God for those who pray it. But Psalm 110 does not deserve its neglect: it is an extremely important psalm, skillfully and vigorously written, and it directs us in prayer that uncenters the self— rescues us from self-centeredness by recentering us in the being and action of God. For those who care about doing something about what is wrong with the world, the consequences of praying this psalm are enormous.

Precision Balancing

The two most important sentences in Psalm 110 are oracles of direct address from God: "The LORD says to my lord: 'Sit at my right hand, till I make your enemies your footstool' " (v. 1) and "The LORD has sworn and will not change his mind, 'You are a priest for ever after the order of Melchize-dek' " (v. 4). The two sentences dominate the psalm and divide it into two precisely balanced parts. David Noel Freedman has made the striking observation that each stanza (in Hebrew) has exactly seventy-four syllables—precision balancing![4]

This framework—"the LORD says . . . the LORD has sworn"
—in itself accounts for its first-century prominence. The
people we know something about via the New Testament
were interested above all else in hearing what God had to
say to them. Their thirst for what they had come to realize
was good news was insatiable. Their appetite for the Word
of God was incessant. They were like Ezra Pound in *Homage
to Sextus Propertius:* "Tell it to me, tell it to me, all of it, I guz-
zle with outstretched ears!"[5]

Does this outline—"The LORD says . . . the LORD has
sworn"—also account for its twentieth-century neglect? The
religious voices that command the largest audiences in our
society are those that are publicists for the ego—the religious
ego, to be sure, but the ego all the same. The deep-rooted,
me-first distortions of our humanity have been institutional-
ized in our economics and sanctioned by our psychologies.
Now we have gotten for ourselves religions in the same style,
religions that will augment our human potential and make
us feel good about ourselves. We want prayers that will bring
us daily benefits in the form of a higher standard of living,
with occasional miracles to relieve our boredom. We come
to the Bible as consumers, rummaging through texts to find
something at a bargain. We come to worship as gourmets of
the emotional, thinking that the numinous might provide a
nice supplement to sunsets and symphonies. We read "The
LORD is my shepherd, I shall not want," and our hearts
flutter. We read "You will not fear the terror of the night,"
and we are tranquilized. We read "He does not deal with us
according to our sins" and decide we have probably been too
hard on ourselves. But when we read "The LORD says . . .
the LORD has sworn," our interest flags and we reach for the
newspaper to find out how the stock market is doing.

We are probably no worse than the people of the first
century in these ways. They did it too. The remarkable thing,
though, is that out of the prevailing religious sensuousness

and opportunism a group of people actually developed a taste for hearing what God had to say on his own terms, so much so that their favorite prayer became one that centered their lives in what God was saying: "the LORD says . . . the LORD has sworn." Praying Psalm 110 brought them to centered attention before the *word* of God and involved their lives in the *work* of God.

Midcourse Adjustments

The centered and centering God of Psalm 110 is emphasized by repetition: "The LORD says . . . the LORD has sworn." The repetition is functional; having caught our attention, it keeps our attention. Nothing is more common in the life of the Spirit than to begin right and to end wrong. We are launched into the way of faith by God's word ("the LORD says"), but then we drift. Midcourse adjustments ("the LORD has sworn") are required to maintain the centering.

The self is persistent. Quietly, subtly, ingeniously, it works itself back to the center. We have professional careers to advance. We have institutional responsibilities to maintain. We have families to feed and lawns to mow. We have causes in which we have invested huge hunks of our identity. At one point we found our center in "the LORD says," but an urgent concern distracted us, or a novel subject engrossed us. We are still, of course, religious, but the religion has gradually become a comforting, steadying background to the center-stage self. We have, unawares, become officious clerks in the house of creation, concerned with the neatness of the bookkeeping but oblivious to the wild and extravagant exchanges of mercy and grace that take place all around as God speaks. We become busybody copy editors to the people around us who are learning to tell the story of God's saving love in their lives: we delete commas, rearrange semicolons, get cranky with the sloppiness of the story that they tell in their breathless but awkward syntax. Then we are ripe for a

midcourse recentering after the manner of Psalm 110: "The
LORD has sworn!"

That without deliberate intent we should let the preoccupations of the self usurp adoration of God is understandable,
but it is not inevitable. That our sense of wonder before
God's centering Word should leak through the sieve of the
everyday is commonplace, but it is not necessary. My friends
Larry and Ruth are farmers in Montana. Their farm is in a
mountain valley. A few miles away, across the valley, a range
of the Rocky Mountains begins its rise and within a few miles
lifts skyward to over 7,000 feet. It is a splendid, jagged border
to their horizon, colored with shifting shades of blue and
green as the sun moves across the sky. I was once standing
in the field visiting with them and said, "What a marvelous
setting for your work! But I suppose that you are so used to
it that you don't even see it anymore." They said, "Oh no,
we're caught breathless several times a day. The beauty keeps
unfolding; every day we're involved in fresh variations of it."
Familiarity does not always breed contempt. But reminders
are needed: "The LORD says . . . the LORD has sworn."

Psalm 110 established its eminence in the early Christian
community by centering the self in the God who speaks.
They knew that they were in a messed-up world and that
something had to be done about it. They also knew that their
good works and good intentions were flawed in such a way
that they only made it worse. And they knew that this did not
disqualify them from the work: they had been drawn into
what God was doing in Christ to establish his will "on earth
as it is in heaven."

How were they to do it? They prayed Psalm 110. It shaped
their understanding of who they were and their place in the
world by what it declared that world to be: when God speaks,
things happen. Genesis 1 had trained them in what to expect.
The word of God is creative: "God said . . . and it was so."
In Genesis 1, God's word makes the world; in Psalm 110,

God's word makes Messiah, the Christ.

Messianism was in the air in the first century. The place was crawling with saviors, miracle mongers and assorted messiahs with blueprints for the world's salvation. Everyone was in on it in one way or another. The place was buzzing with excitement. But there was also bewildering confusion. Who was capable of making sense out of it? Who was qualified to sort out the claims and counterclaims? The great foundation stones of biblical revelation from the Hebrew experience were scattered like rubble. Mixed in were gems from Greece and Rome, Persia and Egypt. How was it possible to discern a coherent truth in the chaos? Religion was "without form and void, and darkness was on the face of the deep."

This was the world into which Jesus of Nazareth was born. Poor, powerless and obscure, he was a most implausible messiah. Then God spoke,

The LORD says to my lord:
"Sit at my right hand,
till I make your enemies your footstool."

A king came into being, one who brings order, beauty, justice, peace. God spoke again,

The LORD has sworn
and will not change his mind,
"You are a priest for ever
after the order of Melchizedek."

A priest was formed, one who puts persons into a whole relationship with God. God spoke the king-priest Messiah into being, just as he had spoken creation into being. The birth, ministry, suffering, death and resurrection of Jesus of Nazareth collected and shaped all the scattered materials of truth and revelation into a recognizable, organic, personal event—a stunning act of redemption.

With the two oracles (vv. 1 and 4) as anchors, the psalm elaborates metaphors rather than arguments to show Messiah drawing, without coercion, hopeful armies to his leadership:

> *Your people will offer themselves freely*
> *on the day you lead your host*
> *upon the holy mountains.*
> *From the womb of the morning*
> *like dew your youth will come to you.*

A second group of metaphors shows God establishing his rule against all opposition:

> *The Lord is at your right hand;*
> *he will shatter kings on the day of his wrath.*
> *He will execute judgment among the nations,*
> *filling them with corpses;*
> *he will shatter chiefs*
> *over the wide earth.*

The final sentence is unforgettable:

> *He will drink from the brook by the way;*
> *therefore he will lift up his head.*

Early Christians saw their Lord Jesus in that figure: the king-priest among us on our level, thirsty in his humanness and kneeling at the brook; then refreshed, with lifted head, proceeding on his way, ruling and saving. The grand and the homely are integrated, the personal and the political are united in that figure.[6]

This rendition of Messiah was far too unprepossessing for the worldly arrogant. They wanted a messiah who would develop power plays that would set the world back on its heels. They dismissed this one with contempt. The image fared no better with the timidly pious. A thirsty, kneeling messiah was too vulnerable and ordinary for them. They wanted a messiah who would get them out of the limitations and humiliations of their everydayness. But for those who were learning to pray, involving themselves in the action of God after the manner of Jesus, the image was exactly right.

Messiah is put together out of the fragmented functions of

ruling and saving, of king and priest. In antiquity (in the person of Melchizedek), the office of king and priest had been a single, organic function. But the functions had gotten separated so that instead of being complementary they were, more often than not, conflicting and competitive rather than coordinated parts of a whole. The king represented God's power to rule, shape and guide life. The priest represented God's power to renew, forgive and invigorate life. The one, associated with the palace, operated in the external world of politics. The other, associated with the temple, operated in the internal world of the spirit. The king specialized in horizontal, human relationships. The priest specialized in vertical, spiritual relationships. The one was responsible for giving structure to life; the other, for giving life to the structure. They were obviously made for each other, but they did not act like it. Then, before the eyes of a few Palestinians, it all came together in the life of Jesus. Psalm 110 describes the coming together in the making of Messiah.

God ruled and saved, and the two acts were the same thing. All the parts of the universe and history fell into place and made sense; all the longings and appetites of the spirit found a terminus. The life without and the life within were demonstrated to be a single life: the life of God in Jesus Christ, Lord and Savior.

Put Together
Then something else happened—if possible, even more wonderful. At the same time that they discovered this putting together and centering of all things in Messiah, they also discovered that they were centered, which is to say, unself-centered. The self, distraught and distracted in attempting to please a hundred gods and avoid a thousand demons, no longer had that impossible task. The self's desperate quest to find answers and acquire knowledge that would establish it in a godlike security was over. The obsessive morality that

people hoped would fit their selves for heaven but only made them miserable to live with was done with. All the gnostic systems and moral sweat and pagan superstitions were thrown out: "Sit at my right hand till I make your enemies your footstool"—the rule was accomplished. "You are a priest for ever after the order of Melchizedek"—the redemption was completed. The *world* was put together so that it made sense; *they* were put together so that they made sense. Psalm 110 shaped the many-dimensioned truths of the Messiah-making Word of God into a prayer that kept the life of faith attentive and responsive to the comprehensive range of what God was doing in each person and in the entire world. No wonder it was their favorite.

An Immodest Agenda

Amitai Etzioni, an immigrant Israeli sociologist, has set forth with urgent passion what he calls "an immodest agenda" in an effort to do something about the precipitous decline of civilization in America. He has abandoned the cool objectivity of his academic discipline and is making a fervent appeal to Americans for a commitment to our common good as a society and a nation. He is convinced that such a commitment must come not from a new social plan or legislative program but from widespread unself-centering. He writes, "It is my thesis that millions of individual Americans, the pillars of a free society and a vigorous economy, have been cut off from one another and have lost their effectiveness. . . . The need to rebuild the economy, national security and the community calls for a social philosophy and an individual orientation that are much less ego-centered."[7] He argues that America must be reconstructed from the ground up by leadership that demonstrates that the self-centered "me-ism" and other pop psychologies of the past decade will not work over the long, American haul.

It *is* an immodest agenda. But not nearly as immodest as

the one Christ set for his followers, who acquired a reputation for turning the world upside down. They discovered very early that only prayer was both personal enough to get them unself-centered and comprehensive enough to include all aspects of the fallen world in the personal/political action of Messiah. The frequency with which they prayed Psalm 110 is evidence of their discovery. Unlike our secular prophets and moralists, they did far more than analyze and urge—they had a workable strategy that they faithfully put into action in their praying. There has not been a day since, when Christians (sometimes few, sometimes many) have not been praying Psalm 110 and prayers like it. Recruits keep getting drawn into the ranks.

God has made it clear that he is not content to rescue a few souls from damnation. Redemption has been conceived on a scale far exceeding our capacity to comprehend it—a new heaven and a new earth are involved. People who pray find themselves involved both with the king who is establishing his rule in the cosmos and the priest who is setting persons right, before God. In prayer we participate from the center to the periphery of God's oscillating personal/political action.

4 Unself-Government

The LORD reigns; he is robed in majesty;
  the LORD is robed, he is girded with strength.
Yea, the world is established; it shall never be moved;
  thy throne is established from of old;
  thou art from everlasting.

The floods have lifted up, O LORD,
  the floods have lifted up their voice,
  the floods lift up their roaring.
Mightier than the thunders of many waters,
  mightier than the waves of the sea,
  the LORD on high is mighty!

Thy decrees are very sure;
  holiness befits thy house,
  O LORD, for evermore.

Psalm 93

The sovereignty that crossed the surf onto the shore of the New World was a new sovereignty. They began the era of absolute human sovereignty—which is to say the era of absolute human presumption. An infinitely greedy sovereign is afoot in the universe, staking his claims.

Wendell Berry[1]

Greek children are raised, I presume, with the conviction that Greece is best. Chinese children probably grow up with similar convictions about their country. Also Tanzanian children. At any rate I know that I was raised with the firm belief that America is best, the land of the free and the home of the brave. I also acquired a vaguely formulated but solidly established belief that America was a Christian place. The extraordinarily beautiful mountains and plains, the vast forests and wild rivers were God's bounty. Childhood and textbook stories gave me the overall feeling that America had a Christian history. George III fit the image of Pharaoh conveniently enough. My ancestors were survivors of malign persecutions, their Atlantic passage a kind of Red Sea event. There were even tribes of hostile barbarians enough like the Canaanites to provide convincing parallels between American Pilgrims and Hebrew children. America was the Promised Land; Americans were God's chosen people.

The government that developed on this promised land by these chosen people was a democracy—self-government. There had been earlier ventures in democracy from time to time, but nothing this thorough or successful. Fashioned in a land that exhibited all the qualities of a promised land among a people who experienced the dignity of a chosen people, it was hardly surprising that democracy was viewed, pure and simple, as God's blessing. The version of history that I was taught said that after living for centuries under the abusive weight of papal domination and after a millennium of threat from Islamic fanaticism, American democracy was too good to be true—yet it was true.

American democracy is, by any account, a great success. If there are critics of the American political system—and there are, some of them extremely strident—they do not ordinarily oppose the concept of self-government but only flaws in its execution or hypocrisies in its institutions. There are, it must be admitted, gaping holes in some of our claims. There are many people for whom the promises have yet to come true. Still, the critics of America do not seem to be standing in line to emigrate to either Cuba or China. After centuries of rule by tribal chieftains, military dictators, kings and queens, councils of wise advisers and cabals of passionate revolutionaries, we have arrived at democracy. Self-government is the apex of political science.

The American Christian with a historical memory so thoroughly shaped by a sense of divine promise and blessing can hardly fail to assume that God's style of government must be along the lines of self-government. But the assumption comes to grief in prayer: there, we find ourselves in a reality quite different from what we grow up in as Americans. The people are not sovereign; God is sovereign. Praying, we do not enter a world where our wishes are fairly represented and then shaped into legislation that balances the maximum of liberty with the minimum of interference. The biblical revelation presents the God to whom we pray as unequivocally sovereign. It also makes clear that God's intention is to exercise his sovereignty in a total, sweeping way. Everything and everyone is subject to him. There is no division of reality into spiritual and material, with God assigned to rule the spiritual and the politicians assigned to the material. God's rule is inclusive and absolute.

The act of prayer, then, involves us in powerful crosscurrents: the swift, noisy, flashing current of assumptions on self-government and the slow, quiet, rising tide of belief in God's sovereignty. We pray prayers of submission to God as king in an atmosphere in which we insist on having a vote in everything. How much does our American pride in self-government unconsciously subvert our Christian commitment to God's sovereignty? Far more, I think, than we are commonly aware. But the subversion also operates in the other direction. Our enthusiastic insistence on self-rule is altered into grateful obedience to God's rule. The cascading mountain stream is absorbed by the rising ocean tide. This has, of course, both personal and political consequences.

The LORD Reigns

Seven psalms proclaim and celebrate this rule.[2] They probably originated in a New Year's Day festival of worship in Israel in which God's sovereign enthronement over the people, the nations, the earth and the year was celebrated.[3] God's rule is pondered and prayed in these psalms with both precision and exuberance. Prayer realizes the pervasive ways in which God's rule interferes with and finally replaces our petty fiefdoms in which we blusteringly try to run our own lives or indolently let others run them. Psalm 93 is prominent among these seven. Regal in its artless simplicity, imposing in its unpretentious brevity, memorable in its strong rhythms, it attracts and convinces. One of the characteristics of Hebrew poetry is that it "rhymes" meanings rather than sounds, paralleling a similar or contrasting meaning in successive lines. This can be shown visually in the opening stanza of Psalm 93 by separating the lines into four pairs of paralleled sense rhymes.

> *The LORD reigns;*
> > *he is robed in majesty;*
> *The LORD is robed,*
> > *he is girded with strength.*
> *Yea, the world is established;*
> > *it shall never be moved;*
> *Thy throne is established from of old;*
> > *thou art from everlasting.*

The four paired lines build a foursquare solidity. God's sovereignty is a structural fort. It is a historical fact as much as a theological fact. It is a political fact as much as a spiritual fact. It is an earthly fact as well as a heavenly fact. People of faith accept and rejoice in this sovereignty. They enjoy its immense benefits. They celebrate its great holidays. They admire and remember its significant leaders. They seek to be responsive to its legislation and to promote its ends.

At the same time, though, we live under other governments. The enthronement of God, prayed in Psalm 93, was prayed by the Hebrews throughout the centuries in which they also regularly enthroned their own kings. For about five hundred years they were a monarchy. Through that half a millennium they crowned forty-two kings.[4] Some of the kings were magnificent; some were awful. Many were no better and no worse than we would expect. But every king was crowned in subordination to God's rule. No king was permitted to think of himself as anything other than a human with a job to do. No citizen was permitted to think anything different.

By crowning their kings in the setting of worship, the ritual and song and prayer shaped the imagination of the people to respond to God, and only God, as sovereign. The kings didn't always remember this, nor did the people. But at least the right foundations were laid. Acts of worship continually returned them to the common conviction that the rule of God was being exercised in the actual political and social community in which they were living. Praying kept them from ever supposing that having a king somehow took precedence over having a God. Such praying has continued unchanged into the era of self-government. Generation after generation of such praying by Jews and Christians has developed such an intricate root system of involvement in the politics of God's rule that no government is safe from challenge or subversion by the community of faith.

It is neither possible nor desirable for people of faith to extricate themselves from the political conditions of the day and live simply and joyously "under God." From time to time, people attempt to form such communities. None of them has worked, either politically or spiritually. The unavoidable reality is that in addition to living under God we at the same time live under a king, a dictator, a prime minister, an emperor, a president or a general with attendant councils, courts, senates, armies, and bureaucracies that see to law and order, conduct the census and dispense justice.

Some rulers claim to have direct access to the mind of God and to be a mirror image of it in their rule. Others acknowledge God's rule in general but believe themselves to be in charge of whatever goes on in *this* nation. Some are so bold as to completely deny God's sovereignty, giving them in effect the final say-so in everything. More often there is simple indifference to God as ruler: God may be believed in as Savior or as comforter, but matters of rule—waging war and collecting taxes, regulating trade and making treaties—are supposed to be far from the mind of God, who has enough to do directing the angels in choir and keeping double-entry accounts in the book of life.

Meanwhile, an underground conviction stubbornly persists: "The LORD reigns." He reigns right here; his throne is earth, the stuff we walk on daily. Furthermore, this rule brooks no opposition: it shall "never be moved." It follows that any earthly leader who is obsessed with exercising power without interference—whether that power is being used to maintain the self unchallenged, or the family in line, or the culture intact, or the government in control—will get more than a little nervous when people are at prayer. Rightly so. The centuries provide more than ample evidence of what happens: a better rule is discerned and embraced in prayer. When the better rule conflicts with the rule of nation, society, family or self, the pray-ers shift loyalties. Some even end up crucified—like Jesus, literally, or like Paul, metaphorically.

But the crucifixions backfire. Instead of getting rid of the challenging rule of God they establish it. These praying people have a long record of being misunderstood by families, imprisoned by governments, fired by employers, ridiculed by culture. But they seem not to mind very much, at least not enough to change their loyalties. They are ruled by a better, wiser, more gracious sovereign and are pleased to continue under that government.

Floods of Unrule

How do they arrive at and maintain such convictions and loyalties? There are long stretches of history that seem to show no signs at all of God's rule. There are passages of personal experience that seem all muddle and disorder. If the rule of God is to be affirmed and obeyed, the frequent and disrupting experiences of "unrule" must also be prayed through.

> *The floods have lifted up, O LORD,*
> *the floods have lifted up their voice,*
> *the floods lift up their roaring.*

What good is it that the earth is established if floods rush savagely across its firm surface? Of what benefit is it that the Lord's throne is established if violent waters ruthlessly wash away everything that is loose, leaving it glistening but bare? What comfort is it that the ground under me is eternally solid if I am swept off my feet and battered by the bruising waves? When the floods come, the earth remains as solid as ever, but nothing else does. The firmament continues, orderly and dependable, but everything between heaven and earth is swept unceremoniously into catastrophe.

In human history the floods grab all the headlines. The established earth has no need to assert itself. It is *there*. Silent. Solid. But the floods lift up their voice, their roaring. The forces of destruction and disintegration, the energies of hurt and disruption, batter and hammer and shout. We can walk for days, years even, on the earth without giving a second thought to its dependable, stoic solidity, but the floods allow no such casual inattentiveness. We can walk all day on dry land and never once notice that we are dry, but if we are swept into the flood we are acutely conscious that we are wet. Dry is our natural state and we take it for granted; wet is an alien state and we panic.

The incredible force of flood waters is awesome. Only the fish who swim in the waters and the birds who fly over the waters are exempt. Floods scour the land. Great trees are uprooted. Immense rocks are shifted. This too-solid earth is scored and recontoured, leaving badlands.

The flood is an initiation into violence; it is also a master metaphor for anarchy. Flood waters have their counterparts in flood passions. The unruliness of passion is notorious. The chaos of lust and greed are inherently chaotic. Human agressiveness is age-old and requires intervening rule. As much as we dislike being told what to do by another, we fear even more a society in which everyone does what is right in his own eyes (Judg 21:25), a nadir that was reached at least once in Hebrew history and not a few other times in world history.

But there has always been a recovery of government. If there had not, there would be no human history. All government is, in one way or another, a response to the floods. If there were no floods there would be no government. Because of anarchy, government is required. If everyone and everything existed in harmonious tranquillity, government would be as questionable as the vermiform appendix.

Floods have analogies in marketplaces, battlefields, families and playgrounds: rules are set, everyone is doing what is expected of them, all are having a good time, and then suddenly a single person goes berserk and the peaceful pursuit disintegrates in a melee of hitting and yelling and looting. Are there no guarantees against it? Is there no way to eliminate the destructive floods? On the land, dams are

built and dikes constructed; in society, governments are
formed, police deployed, legislation enacted. Success varies.
The Noachian flood of judgment was a response in kind to
the flood of violence ravaging the earth: "the earth was filled
with violence" (Gen 6:11, 13), and then, "the waters of the
flood came upon the earth" (7:10). But no more. Violence
will no longer be met with violence: "Never again shall there
be a flood to destroy the earth" (9:11).

> *Mightier than the thunders of many waters,*
> *mightier than the waves of the sea,*
> *the LORD on high is mighty! (Ps 93:4)*

The anarchical floods are matched by the sovereign Lord.
Three times the floods lift up their voice; three times the
Lord's might proves sovereign. These paired triplets resonate
through the biblical memory. The devil's three testings of
Jesus are met and defeated by three sovereign words (Mt 4:1-
11). Peter's three denials are matched by three affirmations
of love (Jn 21:15-19). Paul's three protestations against his
"thorn" are matched by the triple reassurance, "my grace is
sufficient for you" (2 Cor 12:8-9). Luke gives three renderings
of Paul's conversion, countering his thrice-reported terrorist
activities in the early church.[5]

In all these events, God's sovereignty is not merely
asserted, it is experienced. God's rule is not dogma deduced
from concepts of God's omnipotence; it is witness that
articulates the experience of people who have been battered
and wounded but who have gone on to experience God's
rule as "mightier."

This witness has enormous implications, for if God is not
sovereign, I do, in fact, live in chaos. Randomness and
chance permeate the universe. On the other hand, if God
rules, there is foundational order. No accident is sheer
accident. No chaos is ultimate. No conflict is basic. Whatever
other wills, powers and influences that I live under and
among, one is first and last, foundational and final: "The

LORD on high is mighty." Life is not a haphazard affair run by a committee that meets on alternate Tuesdays, each member subject to intense lobbying by special interests and prone to play favorites with friends and family. The world has design and order. I can plan, hope, believe. The confusion and conflict that convulse history are bounded by a larger clarity and peace.

Do reverberations from this prayer sound in the baptism of Jesus? Early Christians observed continuities between the flood waters of judgment, from which Noah was saved and blessed with a new beginning, and the waters of baptism, out of which Jesus emerged for our salvation and established a new covenant. The descent of the Holy Spirit in the form of a dove as Jesus rose from the waters was associated with the dove-delivered evidence of emergent life after the flood. God's blessing to Noah, which included a comprehensive delegation of authority, has a parallel in the heavenly voice to Jesus: "This is my beloved Son" (Mt 3:17). The phrase is a quotation from Psalm 2 and as such is not a term of endearment but a declaration of authority: Messiah emerges from the death-dealing abyss and rules over the chaos. "Mightier than the waves of the sea, the LORD on high is mighty!"

Force Is No Attribute of God
How is this mightier-than-the-waves-of-the-sea rule of God put into effect? How does it enter our history? How is it realized in our lives? Three lines describe how:

Thy decrees are very sure;
holiness befits thy house,
O LORD, for evermore.

Thy decrees are very sure. The waves are subdued by decrees. The violence of the seas is not countered by violence from the skies. "Force is no attribute of God," said Ignatius of Antioch. This is an amazing, but thoroughly biblical, assertion. The means by which God's rule is put into effect is word not muscle, decrees not armies, creative speech not coercive act. These decrees, which can be so casually ignored and so twisted, continue to be spoken age after age by prophet and priest, king and wise man, apostle and disciple. By means of the decrees the rule is maintained.

There is urgent pressure to meet the world's God-defying violence on its own terms—to put it down, to counter brute violence with raw power. "Lord, do you want us to bid fire come down from heaven and consume them?" (Lk 9:54). But God will not be stampeded into acting out of character. His *word* rules: thy *decrees* are very sure. The edicts of God are firm and nothing else is firm. The seemingly fragile word of God is opposed to the arrogant, intimidating actions of the world. The violence and arrogance subside and are spent; the word is firm as ever. *Sure (ne'emnu)* is translated in various contexts as "faithful," "steadfast," "foundational." Another form of the word concludes and confirms prayers: amen, yes, firm and affirmed, very sure.

"Thy decrees" set energies in motion—energies of providence and of redemption—that finally have their way, outlasting the headline-making spasms of violence. Journalists and historians rarely take notice of these decrees, but there are always a few observant, contemplative people who remain attentive. In the same Jerusalem where Psalm 93 was devoutly and defiantly prayed for so many centuries, Amos Oz, a modern Israeli novelist, creates the character of Hannah to give witness to the sovereign energies that continue to operate in that city, unnoticed and unremarked in the international violence and banal secularism. One day she stands at her kitchen window and looks out:

> On a branch of the fig tree which sprouted in our garden a rusty bowl had hung suspended for years. Perhaps a long-dead neighbor had thrown it from the window of the flat above and it had caught in the branches.

It was already hanging covered in rust outside our kitchen window when we first arrived. Four, five years. Even the fierce winds of winter had not brought it to the ground. On New Year's Day, however, I stood at the kitchen sink and saw with my own eyes how the bowl dropped from the tree. No breeze stirred the air, no cat or bird moved the branches. But strong forces came to fruition at that moment. The rusty metal crumbled and the bowl clattered to the ground. What I mean to say is this: All those years I had observed complete repose in an object in which a hidden process was taking place, all those years.[6]

It was not far, a few hundred yards or so, from this place that Psalm 93 had been prayed in New Year's Day celebrations of the Lord's enthronement, the Lord whose "decrees are very sure." Strong forces were at work "all those years." They still are.

A second line describes the way God's rule is perceived: *holiness befits thy house.* "Befits" is a weak translation of *na'wah.* There is a positive, pulsating quality to the word in both its sound and sense: "makes lovely, adorns becomingly." *Na'wah* is quiet as a pulse, strong as a pulse. It is used more frequently in the Song of Solomon than in any other book of the Bible.[7] The context there is the dialog of lovers. In erotic love two powerful and sovereign wills touch and respond. If one will forces another, there is the ugliness of rape. If one will abdicates to the other, there is the dullness of dishrag acquiescence. Only when the two wills are fully developed and expressed in responsive relationship do we acclaim their beauty.

It is understandable that in these dialogs that celebrate the intimacy of human love this word should occur so frequently, but it is a surprise to find it in Psalm 93 that celebrates the rule of God in an unruly world. We expect images of loveliness and beauty in love lyrics, but doesn't rule require a colder context marked by severity and efficiency?

God, it seems, does not abandon his essential character when he rules. A God of steadfast love and deep holiness, he is more himself than ever in his rule. He does not set aside the robes of holy love when he exercises his rule in the mud of human history. The *means* of God's rule are consistent with the *ends* of that rule: *holiness,* the gradual, patient, penetrating beauty of God's rule in our desecrated, violated, profaned world.

O LORD, for evermore. The third line affirms the rule in ordinary time. "As the days stretch out through history" catches the tone of the Hebrew "forever," *l'orek yamim.* This is not God's rule eternal in the heavens apart from human history but God's rule working itself out through the calendar. Prayer is not a patient wait for the rule to come into effect at the end of history, it is patient participation in present rule. God's rule is not being held in reserve to be inaugurated at some future date, after centuries of human rulers have done their best (or worst). It is in operation now. It does not depend on public acknowledgment.

Whether men and women know it or not, they are now living under God's rule. Some live in rebellion that can be either defiant or ignorant. Some live in an obedience that can be either reluctant or devout. But no one lives apart from it. It is the premise of our existence. There are no days when the rule is not in operation. The week is not divided into one Lord's day when the rule of God is acknowledged and six human days in which factories, stock exchange, legislatures, media personalities and military juntas take charge and rule with their lies and guns and money. Nor is the rule restricted to occasional interventions that are later remembered as great historical events—exodus and exile, Christmas and Easter.

It is, of course, not obvious. The decrees of the rule are not audible to unbelieving ears, the beauty of the rule is not visible to unbelieving eyes, the presentness of the rule is not apparent to anxious minds and hurting bodies. But many great and important realities are not obvious: the atomic structure of matter, for instance, or the properties of light, or the complexities of language. All the same, even when we misunderstand or do not understand we continue to pick up objects, see forms and speak words. Likewise, neither ignorance nor indifference diminishes God's rule. Day after day "the LORD reigns." Taking into account the rebellious passions, malicious temperaments and slothful wills of millions of people, along with the good intentions, misguided helpfulness and ill-timed ventures of other millions—not to speak of the disciplined love, purged obedience and sacrificial service of still other millions—our Sovereign presides over and works with all of this material, personal and political. With it and out of it he shapes existence. He seems to be in no hurry. But prayer discerns that leisure is not indolence. Slowness is not slackness. In the end the sovereign will is done.

Now the symmetry is complete: three lines of anarchic violence countered by three lines of the Lord's mightier rule, expounded in three lines of the way the rule is administered.

Concealed Egotism

Thus prayer is subversive activity. It involves a more or less open act of defiance against any claim of ultimacy by the current regime. "Concealed egotism," says Herbert Butterfield, "is perhaps a greater cause of political conflict, a greater source of political problems, than anything else on this globe."[8] Professor of modern history at Cambridge University, Butterfield has spent an erudite career searching out and tracing the historical processes that have resulted in the modern condition. But to him "concealed egotism" is greater than any of them. If he is right, the call to prayer, an act that drags egotism into the open and begins to do something about it, is a major corrective to the political problems of the day.

God rules. Prayer develops in us an awareness of God's rule: his intentions, his ways, his strategies, his commands. Jesus' blunt statement, "He who loves father or mother more than me is not worthy of me" (Mt 10:37), relativizes all authority—family, judicial, cultural, governmental. In praying this prayer an interesting change takes place in us. As our loyalties are detached from nation, club, race or other affiliation, our actual capacity for community increases. Patriotism is often only a bloated egotism. Prayer reduces the stridency of our political protestations but enhances our skills of citizenry—our commitments, our involvements, our values, our passion for social justice. We become aware of God's grand sovereignty in prayer; we also discover a developing inclination to obedience. Slowly but surely, not culture, not family, not government, not job, not even the tyrannous self can stand against the quiet power and creative influence of God's sovereignty. Every natural tie of family and race, every willed commitment to person and nation is finally subordinated to the rule of God.

5 Unself-Help

God is our refuge and strength,
  a very present help in trouble.
Therefore we will not fear though the earth should change,
  though the mountains shake in the heart of the sea;
though its waters roar and foam,
  though the mountains tremble with its tumult.

The LORD of hosts is with us;
the God of Jacob is our refuge.

There is a river whose streams make glad the city of God,
  the holy habitation of the Most High.
God is in the midst of her, she shall not be moved;
  God will help her right early.
The nations rage, the kingdoms totter;
  he utters his voice, the earth melts.

The LORD of hosts is with us;
the God of Jacob is our refuge.

Come, behold the works of the LORD,
  how he has wrought fertility in the earth.
He makes wars cease to the end of the earth;
  he breaks the bow, and shatters the spear,
  he burns the chariots with fire!
"Be still, and know that I am God.
  I am exalted among the nations,
  I am exalted in the earth!"

The LORD of hosts is with us;
the God of Jacob is our refuge.

Psalm 46

In the Christ life nothing, nothing at all, can be purchased at the do-it-yourself shop.

Harry Blamires[1]

A good friend, pastor of a church in Baltimore, was mugged one summer night while walking his dog. His assailant took his watch and wallet and then, just to let him know who was running the show, threw him to the ground and kicked him a couple of times in the ribs. When I saw him a few days later he was bruised, sore and still feeling the emotional effects of the violence. He told me that he was looking forward to leaving the next week for Wyoming, where he would vacation for a month in the Grand Tetons, far from the crime-ridden city.

Six weeks later I met him again. This time his arm was in a sling. "What happened?" He had been riding a horse on a trail in the Wyoming Rockies. The high country there is pristine and exhilarating. There it is impossible to harbor a mean thought for more than ten seconds, let alone act in a mean way. The nearest criminal is at least a hundred miles away as the crow flies. Suddenly, his horse reared, spooked by a shadow, and my friend was on the ground, writhing in pain with a broken arm. He commented, "It is safer to walk on the streets of Baltimore at night than in the mountains of Wyoming in daylight—that wilderness has twenty different ways to kill you."

Each day we wake up to a world of violence. Things are falling apart. People snarl and snap at each other. It isn't safe to walk the city streets at night. But neither is it safe to hike in the wilderness mountains by day. The world is in a bad way: the earth's resources are being used up in an orgy of gluttony; the earth's beauty is being ravaged at an unprecedented rate; the earth's people are being tortured and cursed and demeaned in an epidemic of dehumanization. People compile statistics and publish their findings each year. The numbers are appalling: murders, rapes, assaults, robberies, child abuse, spouse abuse, political terrorism, wars. The cruelties that people think up to inflict on others surpasses our ability to take it in. When we see what people do to each other and to the land we want to leave for the hills. But no sooner do we get there than we find ourselves in the middle of another kind of violence: a volcano erupts and destroys mountains; a flood roars over river banks and drowns a ranch; an earthquake opens a chasm in the earth, toppling everything that is erect and swallowing it in its gorge.

The earth is a violent place. It is violent in city and country. It is violent whenever people get together and it is violent when they don't get together. We want a life where things are safe and comfortable. We want things under control. We want to exclude the evil, the danger, the disaster. We put padlocks on our doors and build fences around our yards. We place policemen on our streets. We build arsenals of weapons and deploy them across the world. For all our efforts the violence does not diminish.

Praying in the Midst of Violence

If violence can neither be escaped nor wiped out by counterviolence, is there anything to do but contain it as best we can and stoically put up with it? There is. We can pray. Wise and respected voices across many centuries tell us prayer is the only act that makes a difference.

Psalm 46 is one of these voices, praying in the midst of violence in order to do something about it. It is our desperately needed corrective to the widespread malpractice of prayer as withdrawal, as escape. When the world dispenses its blows and humiliations a little too liberally, we try to pray ourselves into a private world of consolation where we seek God's sympathy. Set alongside biblical prayer, and in particular alongside Psalm 46, such prayer is seen as a symptom of illness of spirit.

Healthy prayer does not withdraw. But neither does it

confront. It is not so much a way of dealing with what is wrong in the world or myself as a way of dealing with *God* in the world and in myself. Evil (in the form of violence, in Psalm 46) is dealt with indirectly: it is absorbed into the forms and ceremonies of prayer. Prayer frees us from the assault of brute experience by setting us in the energies of grace experience. In the process, the violence itself is changed.

Praying people have been successfully doing this for centuries in every part of the world, and they continue with incalculable impact. That journalists do not report their actions or their effects does not diminish the strength of their persistent peacemaking. Violence is taken seriously but kept in perspective. God requires my attention even more than the violence; in attending to him, I see his city taking shape in the catastrophe.

Violence Without and Within

The background images of Psalm 46 are violent. Praying this psalm puts us in touch with more violence than we bargained for. Three sets of images are used. First, there is violence in nature: the earth opening its jaws in an earthquake,[2] volcanoes erupting out of the ocean, flood waters spilling destruction (vv. 1-3). The next set of images refers to political violence: angry nations, kingdoms that disintegrate, solid achievements of governments melting away like wax figures under a hot sun (v. 6). A third set refers to military violence: wars, bows, spears, chariots—the frightening arsenal of weapons used to hurt and kill, to conquer the weak and enslave the poor (v. 9). It is easy to footnote with contemporary details: earthquakes in Turkey, famine in the sub-Sahara, flood waters on the Mississippi, wars in the Middle East. We are looting the earth's resources. We are aborting the unborn. Violence without; violence within. Some act out their hostilities on others and we put them in prisons. Some act out their hostilities on themselves and we put them in mental hospitals. Some act out their hostilities on nations and we put medals on them.[3]

If we think that prayer is going to get us out of the conflict, we are misinformed. If we think that an immersion in the Psalms will insulate us from the abrasive news of the day, we are mistaken. If we think that looking to God fills us with undisturbed peace and unalloyed joy so that there is simply no space left in our lives for an awareness of barbarity, we are wrong. Nature is violent. Governments are violent. People are violent. Reading the Psalms is a shocking experience. Praying is a courageous act.

But even though the imagery of Psalm 46 is violent, violence is not the subject. *God* is the subject. Whatever the circumstances out of which prayer arises, it deals with God. No matter how God-defiant or God-forsaken the settings in which we find ourselves, prayer, with a kind of built-in radar, tracks its way to God. Nothing can "out-reality" God, and prayer is the primary action in which we cultivate awareness of this unattended and unperceived reality in the midst of the noise and neon.

The LORD of hosts is with us;
the God of Jacob is our refuge

is the heartbeat of this prayer, the two lines marking the systole and diastole of its interior rhythm. The couplet is repeated after each of the three symmetrically composed parts—after verses 3, 6 and 10.[4]

The naming of God is done here with great care. *LORD of hosts* paints a picture: "hosts" are "armies"—vast, angelic troops, swift and fell, carrying out the divine command. *God of Jacob* recalls a story: the persistent assailant at the river Jabbok who wrestled Jacob into the intimacy of blessing. A powerful God, "LORD of hosts," and a personal God, "God of Jacob." But there is a surprising reversal in the way these names are connected with our expectations. We expect the military metaphor to be associated with defense, "refuge."

We expect the personal metaphor to be connected with intimacy, "with us." But the terms are deliberately rearranged so that we get intimacy with the warrior God and defense from the family friend. A powerful God (LORD of hosts) befriends (is with us); a personal God (God of Jacob) protects (is our refuge).

God is one, in any case. The shifting of terms prevents stereotyped expectations of just what God will be and do. Cliché is the great enemy of prayer. The particularities of faith are blurred into generalities through pious repetition. But now our perceptions, and therefore our expectations, are sharp again. In a destructive society, we are treated with dignity (we are not violated). In a depersonalized society, we are engaged in relationship (we are not isolated). We are not things to be used. We are not objects to be ignored. We are valued, protected and honored; we are loved, listened to and spoken with. We experience safety and intimacy. What we have experienced, we can then do. "The LORD of hosts is with us; the God of Jacob is our refuge."

Civilization as We Know It

There is more. The triple affirmation of a powerful and personal God is linked to an image that encourages the praying imagination to realize what this affirmation means in a violently disintegrating world. The image is presented in verse 4:

There is a river whose streams make glad the city of God,
  the holy habitation of the Most High.
God is in the midst of her, she shall not be moved;
  God will help her right early.

In contrast to the pervasive violence that constitutes the atmosphere in which we pray, the city of God is set down as a simple matter of fact. A city is a *civil*ized place, a place of courtesy and trust. It is not exclusively this in our experience, but it is so characteristically (it is the exceptions that get reported). This city of God is not a blueprint for the future, not a hoped-for aspiration and not a promise that just might be enacted with the right legislation. It is here. Now. God dwells in this place, this world. God is not an occasional tourist to our shores. He has set up habitation here, not as a camper but as a citizen: there is a *city* of God. It is in the same world where the violence is, which means that we need not go off looking for God in a quiet, secluded glen.

Augustine used this image of the city of God to develop his exposition of the presence and action of God in the midst of human presence and action, the history of God's ways permeating the history of our ways. He wrote *The City of God* in the rough and tumble of one of the most violent times in our history, when Alaric and the barbarian hordes were streaming out of the north and ravaging Roman civilization. This is not escapist theology but something more like prayed journalism.

The city of God on which Augustine reported cannot be identified with the politics, legislation and judiciary that our journalists report and our scholars study. But it would be very much a mistake to conclude that it is therefore invisible, a "spiritual" reality in the midst of our materiality. It is very much visible, very much historical, very much actual.[5] True, it is not seen by many, but that is not because it is invisible but only because they are not looking in the right direction or do not have their eyes trained to see these actions and this presence. Augustine's concept has been systematically ignored for centuries. But it has not been refuted, nor is it likely to be, for it is developed out of the much-confirmed praying of Psalm 46.

Flowing alongside this city, "there is a river." In the ancient world the important cities were built on the shores of great rivers—Nile, Tigres, Euphrates, Tiber. Rivers flowed out from Eden. A river will flow through new Jerusalem. A river is drink and cleansing and transport. That "there is a river" means that God's habitation in this world is no slum existence. It is not a refugee camp desperately thrown together out of packing boxes and barrels. It is well supplied with a river and is therefore a glad place.

The juxtaposition of river and city requires us to understand God's dwelling among us comprehensively—both that which is created by God's word and that which is constructed by builders' hammers. The presence and action of God in our midst is not perceived any better by banishing the noise of the city so that only a pristine creation (the river) remains. Nor is its perception enhanced by eliminating the wild elements of water and wind so that all that is left are the controlled and measured streets and structures of revelation (the city). God's habitation includes both: mystery and clarity, nature and history, the elemental and the complex, creation and kingdom.

In the context of the terrifying and inescapable violence in nature and nations, an astounding claim is made for this river-city: "she shall not be moved." This verb was used earlier in verse 2, "though the mountains *shake* in the heart of the sea." It is used later in verse 6, "the kingdoms *totter.*" Here it is used for the city that "shall not *be moved*" (v. 5). The word comes from the vocabulary of catastrophe.[6] It is used in the ancient literature of Ugarit in an apocalyptic way, for the total falling apart of everything at doomsday. The mountains fall apart, the kingdoms fall apart, but the city does not. Creation is not safe, civilization is not safe, but God is.

The city of God is safe, not because it is defended, inviolate space but because it is the sphere of God's characteristic action, his *help*. The noun *help* is used in verse 1: "a very present help." Dahood translates it as "help from of old," interpreting "very present" as "having been present always"—a long track record of being present. In other words, there is a history to this helping, with centuries of documentation. God is not a desperately conceived new remedy but a tried and true help, a well-proven help. The verb *help* is used in verse 5: "God will help her right early." "At crack of dawn" is the more literal and far livelier translation of the Jerusalem Bible. We need not muddle through half the day, or half our lives, before God shows up, rubbing his eyes, asking if there is anything he might do for us. He knows the kind of world we live in and our vulnerability in it, for he has taken up habitation in it himself (Jn 1:14). He anticipates our needs and plans ahead. He is there right on time to help, "at crack of dawn."

We are helped: not by taking care of ourselves but by being taken care of; not by garrisoning ourselves behind thick walls of indifference but by risking life in the world with a helping God; not by reducing our lives to the trivial dimensions of a self-help project but by venturing into the unfamiliar and untested polar expanses of grace. The great affirmation and insight of the life of faith is that help is being given all the time.

To the objection "I prayed and cried out for help, but no help came," the answer is "But it did. The help was there; it was right at hand. You were looking for something quite different, perhaps, but God brought the help that would change your life into health, into wholeness for eternity. And not only would it change your life, but nations, society, culture." Instead of asking why the help has not come, the person at prayer learns to look carefully at what is actually going on in his or her life, in this history, its leaders, its movements, its peoples, and ask, "Could this be the help that he is providing? I never thought of *this* in terms of help, but maybe it is." Prayer gives us another, far more accurate way of reading reality than the newspapers. "Think of it!" exclaims Bernanos's country priest, "The Word was made Flesh and not one of the journalists of those days even knew it was happening!"[7]

Behold the Works of the LORD
Two commands direct us from the small-minded world of
self-help to the large world of God's help. First, "Come,
behold the works of the LORD." Take a long, scrutinizing
look at what God is doing. This requires patient attentiveness
and energetic concentration. Everybody else is noisier than
God. The headlines and neon lights and amplifying systems
of the world announce human works. But what of God's
works? They are unadvertised but also inescapable, if we
simply look. They are everywhere. They are marvelous. But
God has no public relations agency. He mounts no publicity
campaign to get our attention. He simply invites us to look.
Prayer is looking at the works of the Lord.

We look. What do we see? We see that "he has wrought
fertility in the earth."[8] The proliferation of life is stunning.
Inattentive to anything but the gaudiest of billboards and
bloodiest of disasters, we wake up and look around. Unpray-
ing, we read only the big print, notice only the megatrends,
observe only the giant wreck. Praying, we see the data stream
in from everywhere. One praying pilgrim, Annie Dillard,
walks out of her front door and tells us what she sees:

> The creator goes off on one wild, specific tangent after
> another, or millions simultaneously, with an exuberance
> that would seem to be unwarranted, and with an aban-
> doned energy sprung from an unfathomable font. What is
> going on here? The point of the dragonfly's terrible lip,
> the giant water bug, birdsong, or the beautiful dazzle and
> flash of sunlighted minnows, is not that it all fits together
> like clockwork—but that it all flows so freely wild, like the
> creek, that it all surges in such a free, fringed tangle.
> Freedom is the world's water and weather, the world's
> nourishment freely given, its soil and sap: and the creator
> loves pizzazz.[9]

We also see that "he makes wars cease to the end of the
earth; he breaks the bow, and shatters the spear, he burns

the chariots with fire!" God is engaged in worldwide disarmament. All the ways in which men and women attempt to forcibly impose their wills on neighbors and enemies are
thrown into the trash heap. Violence does not work. It never
has worked. It never will work. Weapons are not functional.
    The history of violence is a history of failures. There has
never been a won war. There has never been a victorious
battle. The use of force destroys the very reality that is
exercised in its behalf, whether honor, truth or justice. Living
in the kind of world in which we do and being the sinners
we are, we sometimes cannot avoid violence. But even when
it is inevitable it is not right. God does not engage in it.[10]
    A steady, sustained look at God's works sees that our
frantic, foolish arms build-up (whether personal or national,
whether psychological or material) is being subjected to
systematic and determined disarmament. Violent action is
the antithesis of creative action. When we no longer have the
will or the patience to be creative, we attempt to express our
will by coercion. The lazy and the immature account for most
of the violence in the world. But however prevalent violence
is, the person at prayer sees that that is not the way most of
the world, the world of God's action, works. But it takes
energy and maturity to see it and to sustain the vision.

Be Still and Know
The second command is "Be still, and know that I am God."
Be still. Quit rushing through the streets long enough to
become aware that there is more to life than your little self-
help enterprises. When we are noisy and when we are hur-
ried, we are incapable of intimacy—deep, complex, personal
relationships. If God is the living center of redemption, it is
essential that we be in touch with and responsive to that
personal will. If God has a will for this world and we want
to be in on it, we must be still long enough to find out what
it is (for we certainly are not going to learn by watching the

evening news). Baron von Hügel, who had a wise word on most subjects, always held out that "nothing was ever accomplished in a stampede."[11]

And know. The word *know* often has sexual connotations in biblical writings. Adam knew Eve. Joseph did not know Mary. These are not, as so many suppose, timid euphemisms; they are bold metaphors. The best knowledge, the knowledge that is thorough and personal, is not information. It is shared intimacy—a knowing and being known that becomes a creative act. It is analogous to sexual relationship in which two persons are vulnerable and open to each other, the consequence of which is the creation of new life. Unamuno, a Spanish philosopher, elaborates: " 'To know' means in effect to engender, and all vital knowledge in this sense presupposes a penetration, a fusion of the innermost being of the man who knows and of the thing known."[12] The knowing results in a new being that is different from and more than either partner. No child is a replica of either parent; no child is mere amalgamation of parents. There are characteristics of both, but the new life is unpredictable, full of surprises, a life of its own.

This sexual knowing that results in newly created life is the everyday experience that is used to show what happens when we pray: withdrawal from commotion, shutting the door against the outside world, insistence on leisurely privacy. This is not an antisocial act. It is not a selfish indulgence. It is no shirking of public responsibility. On the contrary, it is a fulfilling of public responsibility, a contribution to the wholeness of civilization. It is, precisely, creative: You cannot make love in traffic. For all his marvelous creativity, Michelangelo never painted or drew or sculpted anything that compares with any newborn infant. For all his wide-ranging Renaissance inventiveness, Leonardo da Vinci never faintly approximated what any peasant couple brought forth by simply going to bed together. People who pray give themselves to the creative process at this same elemental, world-enriching, self-transcending place of surprise and pleasure.

Be still and know. Civilization is littered with unsolved problems, baffling impasses. The best minds of the world are at the end of their tether. The most knowledgeable observers of our condition are badly frightened. The most relevant contribution that Christians make at these points of impasse is the act of prayer—determined, repeated, leisurely meetings with the personal and living God. New life is conceived in these meetings.

Prayer is not all we do. Patterns and behaviors develop out of the prayers. Continuing the analogy to the family, there is also child-raising, lawn-mowing and making a living. There is intelligence to be exercised, behavior to be shaped, moral decisions and responsible courage. But if no babies are born, there is no continuation of civilization. Births themselves will not take place if people of faith are not desirous enough of God's love, disciplined enough to leave the world's distractions and leisurely enough to "be still and know."

6 Unself-Assertion

For God alone my soul waits in silence;
  from him comes my salvation.
He only is my rock and my salvation,
  my fortress; I shall not be greatly moved.

How long will you set upon a man to shatter him, all of you,
  like a leaning wall, a tottering fence?
They only plan to thrust him down from his eminence.
  They take pleasure in falsehood.
They bless with their mouths,
  but inwardly they curse.

For God alone my soul waits in silence,
  for my hope is from him.
He only is my rock and my salvation,
  my fortress; I shall not be shaken.
On God rests my deliverance and my honor;
  my mighty rock, my refuge is God.

Trust in him at all times, O people;
  pour out your heart before him;
  God is a refuge for us.

Men of low estate are but a breath,
  men of high estate are a delusion;
in the balances they go up;
  they are together lighter than a breath.

Put no confidence in extortion,
  set no vain hopes on robbery;
    if riches increase, set not your heart on them.

Once God has spoken;
  twice have I heard this:
that power belongs to God;
  and that to thee, O Lord, belongs steadfast love.
For thou dost requite a man according to his work.

Psalm 62

Perhaps the will, at its deepest, does not connote self-assertion and dominance, but love and acquiescence; not the will to power but the will to prayer.

William Barrett[1]

There are vast tracts of undeveloped life in most of us. We have capacities for creativity, for love and for accomplishment that lie fallow. We are dormant in our personal relationships and get pushed around unconscionably. We are timid in our work and get passed over for promotions. We are intimidated in our marriages and get used. We feel futile in our communities, fated to shabby and shoddy service from government and business.

Then, from time to time, a person stands up among us and announces how marvelous it is to simply be human. Impressive scientific documentation proves that even the least of us possesses an incredible brain, rich emotions, highly evolved bodies. That such creatures should sit around timid and mousy is ridiculous. That any one of us should be a doormat or a dishrag is scandalous. We are confronted with the demand that we stand up on our own two feet and take with our own two hands what is our right. The appeals are fervent and revivalistic. The sacred scriptures of psychology, economics and political science serve up no end of texts for sermons on self-assertion. Several decades of such preaching, however, have produced the unexpected: a society bloated and bored. How is it that such an obvious need joined with such a reasonable solution has turned out so badly?

Assertiveness—confident action, zestful initiative—is a basic component for living well. But *self*-assertion distorts the fundamental good and spoils it for human development and community health. Psalm 62 is about assertiveness, but of God not self. It prays a transition from asserting the self to participating in the assertiveness of God.

In prayer, we become aware of and responsive to the assertiveness of God. Prayer discovers that God is in action:

he is not an inert gas, an amorphous mass of idea, an abstract virtue. He is not a remote explanation of the cosmos. He asserts his will in this world of human affairs—in government and creation, on the oceans and in the kitchens, in souls and in society. Many fear that if they abandon the gospel of self-assertion they will collapse into timorous self-doubt. In fact, they experience something quite different.

Silent Waiting

The central motif of this prayer that unselfs assertiveness is marked by a repetition. The repetition is binocular, because verses 1-2 and 5-6 are nearly, but not quite, identical. The controlling sentence is "for God alone my soul waits in silence" (vv. 1, 5).

For God alone. God is not one among many. When we pray we are not covering our bases. Prayer is not a way of checking out a last resort of potential help. We understandably want to explore all the options: we write letters, make telephone calls, visit prospects, arrange interviews. We don't know who might be useful to us at any one time. Of course, we cultivate God. But not in prayer. We try it, but it doesn't work. Prayer is exclusive. Prayer is centering. We find that we can't pray with one eye on the main chance and a side glance for God. Prayer trains the soul to singleness of focus: for God *alone.*

My soul waits. Another will is greater, wiser and more intelligent than my own. So I wait. Waiting means that there is another whom I trust and from whom I receive. My will, important and essential as it is, finds a will that is more important, more essential. While waiting, I discover that there is more reality outside me than inside me, and I take up a position to respond to it. I begin to pray by attempting to manipulate the will of God; I end by putting myself in a position to be moved by his will. There is a kind of waiting that has nothing to do with prayer: opportunistic waiting—

a predatory, disciplined holding back until everything is right
for me to pounce. This is the waiting of a cat stalking a bird
or of a person cannily watching for the opening thrust, the
telling word. That is not prayer-waiting. In prayer we are
aware that God is in action and that when the circumstances
are ready, when others are in the right place and when my
heart is prepared, he will call me into the action. Waiting in
prayer is a disciplined refusal to act before God acts. Waiting
is our participation in the process that results in the "time
fulfilled."

In silence. Silence in prayer is not the absence of sound that
occurs when we run out of things to say. It is not the
embarrassing speechlessness that results from shyness. It is
something positive, something fertile. It is being more
interested in what God will say to me than in getting out my
speech to him. It is a preference for hearing God's word over
saying my word. It is rarely the first thing to take place in
prayer. There are many things I have to get off my chest.
There is much that seems urgent to speak. But having said
them, do I then go off and talk to my friends, run my errands
and get on with my daily business? Talk in prayer is essential
but it is also partial. Silence is also essential. But you wouldn't
know it by listening to the prayers of those who refuse
tutelage in Scripture.

Why is there so much noise in the world? Why do we
chatter so much? In this the most expensively schooled
society in the history of civilization, why is there such a
torrent of verbal garbage? Why do we put up with it? Why
don't we turn off the bluff and bluster of our radios and
televisions and enter into the silence? Is it because we do not
really want to hear the word that will expose the futility of
our self-assertiveness and make us new, that will command
the abandonment of our cozy fantasies for a life of hazard-
ous faith?

Silence is prerequisite to hearing. If we reject silence, our words are reduced to puffing our own shriveled selves. If we talk all the time, or let others talk all the time, our ears and mouths are filled with clichés and platitudes, mindless chatter and pretentious gibberish. In silence language is renewed. In the absence of human sound it becomes possible to hear the *logos,* the word of God that gives shape and meaning to our words.

History and Hope

Two reasons support this motif action, and the reasons complement each other. The first is that "from him comes my salvation" (v. 1); the second, that "my hope is from him" (v. 5). The first understands that the past (salvation) gives content to the present. The second is convinced that the future (hope) gives shape to the present. Self-assertion teeters on the thin line of the contemporary. Prayer broadens that line into time-spaciousness, developing a familiarity with the past and a friendliness to the future. Neither persons nor nations can exist in a healthy state absorbed in novelty and defined by advertising. We require a history of salvation and a hope of a kingdom. We need a past and a future that impinge on the present and give it dimensions—depth and height and breadth. Prayer develops these dimensions. Without prayer the past becomes nostalgia and the future fantasy. Self-assertion plunders the past to gratify whims and in so doing destroys its uniqueness, or it greedily mortgages the future to pay for immediate indulgence regardless of the consequence to coming generations.

I Shall Not Be Greatly Moved

A further basis for this radical repudiation of the gospel of self-assertion, this refusal to assert the self in deference to the God who asserts himself, is a condition that is doubly confirmed in experience: "He only is my rock and my salvation, my fortress; I shall not be greatly moved" (v. 2). The three nouns—rock, fortress, salvation—make a triangle of God-assertiveness. The assertions furnish the self's foundation (rock), defense (fortress) and wholeness (salvation). The triangle establishes God as the environment in which the self is affirmed and furnished with the conditions for freedom: stability, integrity, vigor.

The consequence of living in these conditions is a stronger-than-ever sense of self: "I shall not be greatly moved." This is the same word that was used in Psalm 46 as an attribute of the city of God—incapable of being toppled even in doomsday catastrophe (see chap. 5). A self that denies itself, it seems, is not anemic and spindly. Unself-assertion is not wallflower piety. There is something healthy going on here connoting solidity and strength. In contrast, self-assertion turns out to be not self-assertion at all but *impulse* assertion. The self wants to be excited, entertained, gratified, coddled, reassured, rewarded, challenged, indulged. There are people on hand to manipulate and market these impulses by seduction and persuasion. The American self characteristically chooses advertisers instead of apostles as guides. Self-assertion is, in fact, a euphemism for a way of life dominated by impulse and pressure. The self is alternately moved from within by whatever occurs in the emotions and glands, from without by whatever is presented by fashion and fad. As we become practiced in prayer we are unmoved by such bagatelles.

Sagacious and Sober

Appended to each of these unself-assertions are reflections on the way things are in the world of self-assertion. The reflections are sagacious and sober. They keep prayer in touch with a predatory society that does not pray but pushes and plunders, for prayer is not restricted to the way in which we nurture our relationship with God. It is also the way in which we maintain an undistorted, unillusioned view of the prayerless world that is always trying to pressure us into its mold.

The first reflection (vv. 3-4) discerns the base motives that are hidden behind the smiling encouragement of the people who invite us to get ahead in the world.

How long will you set upon a man to shatter him, all of you,
    like a leaning wall, a tottering fence?
They only plan to thrust him down from his eminence.
    They take pleasure in falsehood.
They bless with their mouths,
    but inwardly they curse.

These people are always telling us that they want us to develop ourselves, to do our best, to make the most of our chances. In fact, they are lying to us. They use the bait of our supposed self-interests to hook us for their schemes. What they are really trying to do is get us to serve them so that we can gratify *their* obsession with power, *their* lust for dominance. "They bless with their mouths, but inwardly they curse" (v. 4). What they *say* makes us feel terrific—the whole world is open before us. What they *do* entangles us in dehumanizing anxieties that reduce us to puppets moved by the strings of economics. They are unrelenting pressure against the self and are not satisfied until they have us where they can use us: "How long will you set upon a man to shatter him, all of you?" (v. 3).

The second reflection (vv. 9-10) is a warning against the cynical division of society into the categories of the bad people who win and the good people who lose, the robbers and the robbed.

Men of low estate are but a breath,
    men of high estate are a delusion;
in the balances they go up;
    they are together lighter than a breath.
Put no confidence in extortion,
    set no vain hopes on robbery;

if riches increase, set not your heart on them.

In a world characterized by self-assertion, there is inevitably a great deal of competition and conflict. Everyone is either a winner or a loser. Some get rich and some get poor. Some get all the prizes and some get all the chores. If we let that picture of the world interpret life, we will do one of two things: we will envy the rich or feel sorry for the poor. Some people manage to do both. Envy makes us discontent and changes us from persons into consumers. Pity sentimentalizes us and changes us from persons into bleeding hearts. Eventually we identify with one of the two groups, asserting our status, whether of good luck or bad, as proof of significance. But such an interpretation of humanity is as facile as it is unreal: "Men of low estate are but a breath, men of high estate are a delusion; in the balances they go up; they are together lighter than a breath."

Our electronic, computerized scales do not provide the right image. We have to imaginatively reconstruct the scales of the ancient world. Two pans are hung from the ends of a crossbar that is balanced on a pivot. Do you want to weigh a pound of rice? Place a one-pound weight in one pan. It descends to the ground. But as you scoop rice into the other pan the matched weight lifts it until the pans are even, balanced. Anything can be weighed that way. All that is required is weights to balance against commodities: a one-ounce weight, an eight-ounce weight, a one-pound weight, a five-pound weight. Now we are ready for the psalmist's picture: in one pan put a weight marked "human being, whole self, image of God." In the other pan, put the richest people we know, wealthy with stuffed wallets and safe-deposit boxes full of securities. What happens? Surprise! They go *up* in the balances, contrary to all expectation. There is no weight to them at all: "men of high estate are a delusion." Or, take the most tragic people we know, the ones who have been discriminated against and victimized. Surely these people, deprived of this world's rewards and goods and ennobled by their suffering, are the *real* people. Cruel exploitation has conferred the status of authenticity on them. Put these people on the scales. What happens? Again, surprise! "Men of low estate are but a breath." Self-assertion is futile either way. We do not gain significance by flaunting our victimization or parading our trophies. Tragedy is not proof of significance; accomplishment is not proof of significance. Glorification of victims is as much out of place as adulation of winners. We are only ourselves when we are in a trust relationship with God, defined and commanded by his Word, participating in his power: "Trust in him at all times, O people; pour out your heart before him" (v. 8).

The silence that makes it possible to hear God speak also makes it possible for us to hear the world's words for what they really are—tinny and unconvincing lies. The bravado and promise of self-assertion is sheer puffery.

Quitting the Game
Self-assertion turns society into a game in which corporate greed competes with private indulgence. Political and economic policies limit extreme behavior and enforce some restraint, but the game itself is honored with all the uncritical reverence of a national sport. But a significant and influential number of people have quit playing the game. They are not playing because they are praying. They are praying because

Once God has spoken;
   twice have I heard this:
that power belongs to God;
   and that to thee, O Lord, belongs steadfast love.
For thou dost requite a man according to his work.

"Power belongs to God!" This is maddening and frustrating to the players. They view it as unpatriotic. Nonparticipation interrupts the rhythm of the game. Peter Berger has shown the extensive sociological implications of what happens when people withhold their cooperation with history. "If one cannot transform or sabotage society, one can withdraw from it inwardly. Detachment has been a method of resistance to social controls at least since Lao-tzu and was made into a theory of resistance by the Stoics. . . . The ingenuity human beings are capable of in circumventing and subverting even the most elaborate control system is a refreshing antidote to sociologistic depression."[2]

Every act of prayer both detaches us from the gears and pulleys of self-assertion and throws a monkey wrench into the machinations of the national madness. Space and silence are prepared in which wholeness can germinate and sprout.

Humility (which is the old name for unself-assertion) is probably the least sought-after virtue in America. Mostly, it is despised. At best it is treated with condescension, which is perhaps permissable among the timorous devout who have no aptitude for the affairs of this world. But for centuries, humility was the most admired, if not the most practiced, of the virtues. Can so many whom the world has counted wise be wrong?

Our ancestors believed that humility was the human spirit tempered and resilient and strong. They knew that it was difficult. They knew that even those who admired and professed it were highly prone to subverting it in practice. John Henry Newman is trenchant on the subject: what we usually see, he says, is "a stooping forward unattended with the slightest effort to leave by a single inch the seat in which we are so firmly established. It is an act of a superior, who protests to himself while he commits it that he is superior still, and that he is doing nothing else but an act of grace towards those on whose level, in theory, he is placing himself." He goes on to comment that "humility is one of the most difficult of virtues both to attain and to ascertain. It lies close upon the heart itself, and its tests are exceedingly delicate and subtle. Its counterfeits abound."[3]

But in America even the pretense to humility has been abandoned. We are led off to assertiveness-training workshops and enrolled in management-by-objectives seminars. We are bombarded with techniques by which we are promised to be able to make an impact on society. Nearly all of them turn out to be appeals, in ways subtle or crass, to pride.

It is probably unwise to launch a frontal attack. But through the prayer of Psalm 62 we flank the enemy and practice a life that is lived lightly and cheerfully, without the enormous baggage of bluff and bravado that the self-assertive lug around to mask their weakness. For unself-assertion has nothing to do with the doggy self-effacement that D. H. Lawrence so fiercely repudiated.[4] It is energetic, confident, alert, relaxed. The issue is not *whether* things get done but *who* gets them done, God or me.

What is better for the nation? To encourage 200 million citizens to assert themselves (which in practice means the assertion of greed and ambition)? Or, believing that God is already asserting a far better will in countless visible and invisible ways in a complex working out of salvation in every level of economy and society and culture, to put myself at the disposal of that will because "power belongs to God." Prayer is action that builds a bridge across the chasm of self-assertion to a life of humility, which means getting more interested in and excited about what God is doing than in figuring out what I can do to express myself or improve the world. Such acts are major, albeit unobtrusive, contributions to the commonweal.

7 Unself-Pity

I cry aloud to God,
  aloud to God, that he may hear me.
In the day of my trouble I seek the Lord;
  in the night my hand is stretched out without wearying;
  my soul refuses to be comforted.

I think of God, and I moan;
  I meditate, and my spirit faints.

Thou dost hold my eyelids from closing;
  I am so troubled that I cannot speak.
I consider the days of old,
  I remember the years long ago.
I commune with my heart in the night;
  I meditate and search my spirit:
"Will the Lord spurn for ever,
  and never again be favorable?
Has his steadfast love for ever ceased?
  Are his promises at an end for all time?
Has God forgotten to be gracious?
  Has he in anger shut up his compassion?"
And I say, "It is my grief
  that the right hand of the Most High has changed."

I will call to mind the deeds of the LORD;
  yea, I will remember thy wonders of old.
I will meditate on all thy work,
  and muse on thy mighty deeds.

Thy way, O God, is holy.
  What god is great like our God?
Thou art the God who workest wonders,
  who hast manifested thy might among the peoples.
Thou didst with thy arm redeem thy people,
  the sons of Jacob and Joseph.

When the waters saw thee, O God,
  when the waters saw thee, they were afraid,
  yea, the deep trembled.
The clouds poured out water;
  the skies gave forth thunder;
  thy arrows flashed on every side.
The crash of thy thunder was in the whirlwind;
  thy lightnings lighted up the world;
  the earth trembled and shook.
Thy way was through the sea,
  thy path through the great waters;
  yet thy footprints were unseen.
Thou didst lead thy people like a flock
  by the hand of Moses and Aaron.

Psalm 77

We celebrate not our sickness but our cure.

St. Gregory Nazianzus[1]

Pity is one of the noblest emotions available to human beings; self-pity is possibly the most ignoble. Pity is the capacity to enter into the pain of another in order to do something about it; self-pity is an incapacity, a crippling emotional disease that severely distorts our perception of reality. Pity discovers the need in others for love and healing and then fashions speech and action that bring strength; self-pity reduces the universe to a personal wound that is displayed as proof of significance. Pity is adrenalin for acts of mercy; self-pity is a narcotic that leaves its addicts wasted and derelict.

The contrasts are obvious. They are verifiable in any random home, business, factory, school or playground. The attractiveness of pity and the ugliness of self-pity are unarguable. Yet we live in a society in which self-pity far exceeds pity. The excessively popular genre of literature, the celebrity autobiography, that smothers us in self-pitying subjectivism is the unpleasant evidence that we may be the most self-pitying populace in all of human history. Feeling sorry for yourself has been developed into an art form. The whining and sniveling that wiser generations ridiculed with satire is given best-seller status among us.

There is just enough injustice and disappointment, unfairness and hurt in any person's life to provide ample raw material for the injured imagination to work up into lush melodramas of self-pity. With the stimulus of celebrities who go public with their self-pity and the sanction of a culture that wallows in it, it is easy to make a habit of it.

The great social evil of self-pity is that it takes energies that in their healthy state motivate acts of healing, liberation and enlightenment, and spills them in the sand of the self. The compassion needed for the healing of society ends up as nothing more than a damp, disfiguring stain on the soul.

Self-pity almost always deals with accurate facts: that man does have a better car than I do; that woman does have a more considerate husband than I do; that person does have a better digestive system than I do; that less competent worker got a far better promotion than I did. The facts are not in dispute. The poison is secreted from the invidious comparisons. I find out a truth about myself and compare it to what I learn of another. This knowledge could become a stimulus for growth or an incentive to bless the other. More often, though, it provokes envy. I discover inequalities and injustices. I find the other is richer, better looking, better off, better paid. I feel gypped. I have picked up the germ of self-pity and am infected with one of the most vicious diseases of the ego. Self-pity is viral unhappiness. We are in an epidemic of it. How can we be cured?

The antidote is well known if not well practiced. It is, simply, prayer. Prayer is an act that is sensitive enough to be in almost constant touch with self-pity but strong enough not to become absorbed by it. The initial impulse to pray often comes from self-pity. We feel sorry for ourselves and, because God is widely known to be pitying ("like as a father pities his children, so the Lord pities those who fear him"), we enlist him in feeling sorry for us. But it doesn't work that way. In prayer our self-pity meets up with a stronger, healthier energy and gets itself transformed.

Psalm 77 is a prayer in which maudlin self-pity is unselfed. The psalm falls into two nearly equal but contrasting parts, verses 1-10 and 11-20. The first section is unmitigated and obstinate self-pity. The second section is vigorous and gracious compassion. It is pity, but pity that is thoroughly unselfed.

The Tyranny of the Self
All the typical and unattractive elements of self-pity are on

display in the first half of the psalm. Self-pity, for instance, exaggerates extravagantly. The opening line signals the hysterical quality of the lament: "I cry aloud to God, aloud to God, that he may hear me." The repetition of *aloud* (in Hebrew, the emphatic first word in each phrase) puts the focus squarely on "my trouble." "My soul refuses to be comforted." Why refuse comfort? The refusal betrays the hidden agenda of the lament: using misery as a way of asserting the tyranny of the self. You must notice me because I hurt. My trouble, loudly and dramatically proclaimed, demands that you notice me. Psychiatrist Harry Stack Sullivan quipped that the outstanding trait of such people is that "no lily is good enough; it must always get a little extra verbal paint."[2] "I think of God," but I don't think of him very long, for the consequence is that "I moan." God is a pious pretext to feel sorry for myself in a religious and therefore, presumably, a justified way.

Self-pity is accusing. The all-absorbing trouble leaves no time even for sleep. This sleeplessness is promptly blamed on God: "Thou dost hold my eyelids from closing" (v. 4). The word translated "eyelids" occurs only here in the Bible and may mean "watches" or "vigils." In that case the metaphor is even bolder: "Thou dost seize the watches of my eyes."[3] A pastoral people set watches throughout the night to guard their flocks. The shepherds took turns at the watches, three hours at a time. No one stayed awake through the entire night—or if he did, it would be because someone forcibly seized his eyelids and held them open. My insomnia, in other words, is God's fault. This is a recurrent characteristic in self-pity: someone else, often God, is responsible for my trouble.

Self-pity grovels in nostalgia: "I consider the days of old, I remember the years long ago" (v. 5). The grass was greener fifty years ago. The previous generation was more energetic, more noble, more just. Almost everybody agrees that things

were better in the old days—but no two people agree on
when the old days were. Russell Baker calls our bluff:
"Despite universal yearning for the old days—it is also true
that 99 people out of 100 people who prefer the old days
wouldn't dream of going back unless they could take their car
with them."⁴ Self-pity, a shabby historian, considers and
remembers the past only to feed the injustice of the moment
and to avoid doing anything about it.

Self-pity is morbidly introspective: "I commune with my
heart in the night; I meditate and search my spirit" (v. 6).
There is a healthy self-awareness and a healthy self-study. It
is no virtue to be oblivious to the self, unheeding of the inner
life. But introspection in order to be useful and healthy
requires discipline and guidance; otherwise, as here, it loses
its way in the swamp of self-pity. The self meditating on the
self is in a room without air, without oxygen. Left there long
enough, breathing its own gases, it sickens.

Self-pity is theologically ignorant: "Will the Lord spurn for
ever, and never again be favorable?" (v. 7). This question
launches a series of questions, five of them, that moves to a
climax. The questions involve God but are not addressed to
God. They are rhetorical questions thrown out to the world
at large, a world expected to confirm their self-evident truth.
A rhetorical question assumes agreement. The evidence is so
obvious that no thinking person would dissent. Recasting the
five rhetorical questions as positive statements, they read: (1)
The Lord will spurn forever and never again be favorable;
(2) his steadfast love has ceased forever; (3) his promises are
at an end for all time; (4) God has forgotten to be gracious;
and (5) in anger God has shut up his compassion.

A rejecting God, a tired God, a stingy God, a forgetful God,
an angry God. Can anyone with even a first-grade knowledge
of the God revealed in Scripture and experienced in the
centuries of salvation history support such statements? The
statements are based on neither revelation nor observation;

they are fabricated out of self-pity. No one cares about me. I was born too late to get in on the promises. I have been overlooked. No one feels sorry for me. These details are then expanded into a cosmic proclamation: God has rejected me.

The questions, reeking with self-pity, produce a conclusion in which ignorance competes with bathos: "It is my grief that the right hand of the Most High has changed" (v. 10). Who says that God is loving, compassionate and kind? If he was at one time, he is no longer. *I* am the evidence. My condition, as everyone can see, is proof that God is not what he is reputed to be; otherwise, why would I be so miserable? My grief has a theological basis: God doesn't love me.

The Magnification of Grace

Then, just when we think we can take no more of this, there is a change, a shift, and we are suddenly in an entirely different world. These things happen in prayer. They happen without apparent transition. At one moment we are floundering in a slough of self-pity; the next, we are sure-footed in the mountains, dazzled by the wonders of redemption. The pivot is in the following sentences:

I will call to mind the deeds of the LORD;
  yea, I will remember thy wonders of old.
I will meditate on all thy work,
  and muse on thy mighty deeds.

Four verbs are used to express attentiveness: *call to mind, remember, meditate, muse.* Another set, noun phrases this time, name the object of the attentiveness: *deeds of the LORD, wonders of old, thy work, thy mighty deeds.* The striking thing here is that the four verbs have been in use already in the first half of the psalm (I think, I meditate, I consider, I remember, I commune, I meditate), but the noun phrases are new. The change comes not when we learn to meditate but when we learn on *whom* to meditate. There has been no lack of meditation. There has been no reluctance to direct the mind and spirit inward, beneath the surface of life. The first half of the psalm is meditative, but the meditation is either unfocused ("I meditate" without an object, v. 3) or nostalgic (v. 5) or self-indulgent (v. 6). It is meditation on the injured self. But the moment that meditation shifts from "my trouble" to "thy work" there is a sea change.

What happens in prayer is that an awareness develops: a lot more is going on in the world than I am conscious of when I am disappointed, or hurt, or frustrated, or embittered. The feelings that I have at any one moment, while important and actual, cannot be interpreted accurately apart from the context of God's action. Meditation is an intensification of awareness, of perception. When the focus of meditation is narrowly bound by feelings of self-pity, the self in isolation, the result is an intensification of misery. But if the focus is on God in the self, on God in history, on God in creation, the result is a magnification of grace: "Thy way, O God, is holy" (v. 13). The working of wonders, the manifestation of might, the redemption of people (vv. 14-15) loom on the horizon. I live in a world dominated by creation, by revelation, by redemption. My feelings find their place in the context of God's action and can be interpreted and evaluated accurately. Annie Dillard, in her incomparably expansive meditation on "all thy work," *Pilgrim at Tinker Creek,* shows the result: "Like Billy Bray I go my way, and my left foot says 'Glory,' and my right foot says 'Amen': in and out of Shadow Creek, upstream and down, exultant, in a daze, dancing, to the twin silver trumpets of praise."[5]

Singing Salvation

From this broad panorama a single event is selected and held up for consideration: the exodus out of Egypt (vv. 16-19). That was a time when the natural and the supernatural, the earth and the heavens, the personal and the national, were orchestrated in a single coherent act of redemption.

The event is remembered audio-visually and kinetically: big sounds and flashing lights are set to rhythms that move us to awed praise. We are jolted out of the circular grooves of self-pity that spiral inward and placed in the parade of praise, the way of God's salvation.

> *When the waters saw thee, O God,*
>> *when the waters saw thee, they were afraid,*
>> *yea, the deep trembled.*
>
> *The clouds poured out water;*
>> *the skies gave forth thunder;*
>> *thy arrows flashed on every side.*
>
> *The crash of thy thunder was in the whirlwind;*
>> *thy lightnings lighted up the world;*
>> *the earth trembled and shook.*
>
> *Thy way was through the sea,*
>> *thy path through the great waters;*
>> *yet thy footprints were unseen.*

The very rhythms of the prayer change at this point. Up until now the poetry has been arranged, for the most part, in two-line stanzas. Now the stanzas are composed in stately, sagalike, three-line groupings. The diapasons are called in. Undertones of Genesis 1 are built into the imagery to give a cosmic dimension to salvation. The watery chaos out of which God fashioned a good creation is echoed in these sentences that sing salvation. Both the world we live in (creation) and the world that lives in us (salvation) is God-shaped. Can my formless, watery self-pity be exempt from such power?

Everyone knows that it happened. The very existence of Israel was proof and documentation of the event. Yet no one quite knows how it happened: "thy footprints were unseen" (v. 19). Footprints made in deep waters leave no trace. We live with the consequences of salvation, but that which made it happen is invisible. There is no tangible, visible proof that it happened—except for my very existence right now and the existence of everything great and holy and wonderful.

An Image at Hand
A single word, repeated at the beginning and at the end of
the psalm, shows both the apparent similarity and the actual
difference between the pity that we feel for ourselves and the
pity that God feels for the world and then acts on in
salvation. The word is *hand.*

Its first use is subjective, what *I* feel: "In the day of my
trouble I seek the Lord; in the night my *hand* is stretched out
without wearying; my soul refuses to be comforted" (v. 2).
The Hebrew text is more blunt than the translation indicates:
"My hand runs into the night." The coincidence of *hand* and
run is comical, forming an arresting cartoon image of a hand
running out into the night, looking for help. But another
image is possible. *Hand* is used metaphorically in a great
many ways in the Hebrew language. There is a possible
metaphorical use here that fits the context. It may mean
"wound," as in Job 23:2. Then the image would be of a
running sore; a stinking, suppurating wound; a wound that
isolates and that no one wants to deal with, like that of the
luckless Philoctetes of Greek legend. Not until this wound is
dealt with for what it is—in this case, malodorous self-pity—
can salvation be said to be accomplished.

Its final use is objective: "Thou didst lead thy people like
a flock by the *hand* of Moses and Aaron" (v. 20). It is not quite
what we expect. If a hand is outstretched in the first verse,
we anticipate that it will be grasped or held by the time we
arrive at the last verse. Or, if we begin with a running wound,
we expect to finish with a healing. But that is not what we
get: self-pity is not pressure that extracts concessions from
the Almighty. Rather, it is an occasion that God uses to work
in our largely self-generated misery to bring about *his*
pleasure, which we are surprised to find is also our pleasure.
The hand stretched out in self-pity is answered by the

hands of Moses and Aaron. Their hands do not protect people from trouble but train them in the midst of it. They do not hold the hands of the people, sympathizing with them over their loss of home and security in Egypt. They take their hands and lead them into the harsh desert. The redemption has already been accomplished (by the "arm" of the Lord, v. 15). Now the life of faith must be learned. A life of compassion must be nurtured. This can only be done in the midst of hurt and pain, where wisdom is inaccessible to self-pity. God does not answer our self-pitying request but our need for unselfing. He enters our lives and provides prophet and priest to lead us into and through the wilderness of temptation and trial. Only then can we learn the ways of providence and discover the means of grace—a long, difficult, mercy-marked, grace-guided forty years that represents the middle of the journey for persons who live by faith. It is a journey through which we learn personal morality and social responsibility. Salvation is put to the work of building community, engaging in worship, encountering evil.

The Right Place
Dead-ended as self-pity is, prayer does not forbid it. Any place is the right place to begin to pray. But we must not be afraid of ending up some place quite different from where we start. The psalmist began by feeling sorry for himself and asking questions that seethed with insolence. He ended up singing an old song proclaiming might and grace.

We meditate on our wounded humanity and casually introduce the name of God into our meditations: it is not long before our fainting imaginations are quickened by fearful waters and the trembling deep, by God passing unseen through the crashing thunder and trampling a shaking earth illuminated by lightning gashes, by God redeeming his people and leading them like a flock. Wrested from morbid introspection, we see clouds pouring water and hurling bolts of fire. God is acting for people in need. It is not when we suppress our self-pity, when we still its cry, but when we offer it to God that our whimpering gets gathered into the thunder of his action and becomes a spirit-renewing meditation on God's might, a compassion-exciting participation in God's help. The tiresome "I think of God, and I moan" in the course of prayer becomes the exhilarating "I will meditate on all thy work, and muse on thy mighty deeds. Thy way, O God, is holy. What god is great like our God?"

8 Unself-Righteous

The fool says in his heart, "There is no God."
  They are corrupt, they do abominable deeds,
  there is none that does good.

The LORD looks down from heaven upon the children of men,
  to see if there are any that act wisely,
  that seek after God.

They have all gone astray, they are all alike corrupt;
  there is none that does good,
  no, not one.

Have they no knowledge, all the evildoers
  who eat up my people as they eat bread,
  and do not call upon the LORD?

There they shall be in great terror,
  for God is with the generation of the righteous.
You would confound the plans of the poor,
  but the LORD is his refuge.

O that deliverance for Israel would come out of Zion!
  When the LORD restores the fortunes of his people,
  Jacob shall rejoice, Israel shall be glad.

Psalm 14

The golden apple of selfhood, thrown among the false gods, became an apple of discord because they scrambled for it. They did not know the first rule of the holy game, which is that every player must by all means touch the ball and then immediately pass it on. To be found with it in your hands is a fault; to cling to it, death. But when it flies to and fro among the players too swift for eye to follow, and the great master Himself leads the revelry, giving Himself eternally to His creatures in the generation, and back to Himself in the sacrifice, of the Word, then indeed the eternal dance "makes heaven drowsy with the harmony."

C. S. Lewis[1]

The atheist is not always the enemy. Atheists can be among a Christian's best friends. Atheists, for instance, whose atheism develops out of protest: angry about what is wrong with the world, they are roused to passionate defiance. That a good God permits the birth of crippled children, that a loving God allows rape and torture, that a sovereign God stands aside while the murderous regime of a Genghis Khan or an Adolf Hitler runs its course—such outrageous paradoxes simply cannot be countenanced. So God is eliminated. The removal of God does not reduce the suffering, but it does wipe out the paradox. Such atheism is not the result of logical (or illogical) thought: it is sheer protest. Anger over the suffering and unfairness in the world becomes anger against the God who permits it. Defiance is expressed by denial. Such atheism is commonly full of compassion. It suffers and rages. It is deeply spiritual, in touch with the human condition and eternal values.

Ivan Karamazov is the most famous literary presentation of this atheism of passionate protest. He carried around a notebook in which he copied down every instance of innocent suffering that he heard or read of. There were terrible things in his notebook: accident and torture, cruelty and agony, malignity and despair. He specialized in the suffering of innocent children. The accumulated anecdotes served up an unanswerable indictment against the existence of God: because this is the way the world is, there cannot be a God.[2] But he was always talking about the God in whom he did not believe. He was haunted by the Christ that he rejected. His very atheism was a grappling with the holy, with love, with meaning. His atheism had far more spiritual depth than the conventional pietism of people who burn incense to mask the world's stink of suffering and cheerfully sing tunes about the sunshine of God.

There is another kind of atheism that is a struggle for intellectual honesty. These persons begin with an idea of God formed out of bits of misinformation, fragments of fantasy gathered randomly from movies, talk shows and bull sessions. One day they take a look at the image and decide that God does not have a beard. No beard, no God. Adolescents often become this kind of atheist. With their maturing intellect they re-examine the childish idea of God that they have been carrying around and conclude that it is inadequate. "No intelligent adult could believe in *that*" they say, quite rightly. They become instant atheists. What they fail to ask is, "Are there people of well-developed minds and carefully trained intellects who believe in God? And if they do, what does that belief consist of?"

Pastors encounter this kind of atheism fairly often. My response is to probe further. I ask, "Tell me about this God that you don't believe in. What is he like?" After listening to what follows, I usually can agree: "I don't believe in that God either. Given the material as you present it, I also am an atheist."

I usually have a partner in conversation by this time and am permitted to continue. "Did you know that in the first century one of the common accusations against Christians was that they were atheists? There were hundreds of gods in that culture that Christians did not believe in. They found it uproariously ridiculous that anybody would take those so-called gods and goddesses seriously.

"The pagans were understandably offended when their comforting superstitions and entertaining stories were treated with derision. They also worried that if Christian unbelief caught hold the entire social and political order would be subverted. So Christians were persecuted, imprisoned and sometimes killed on the charge of atheism. That they believed in one God hardly counted as *religious* in a culture where everyone else believed in at least a couple of hundred. Besides, it was hard for the Romans and Greeks to take a god seriously who was a Semitic nobody with neither statues nor temples to represent his presence and validate his importance.

"So you are in good Christian company if there is a god, or gods, that you don't believe in. Would you be interested in talking about that one God those early atheists did believe in?"

These kinds of atheism can be treated with appreciation and respect. The passionately protesting atheist, sensitive to suffering, can be welcomed as a partner in a spiritual and moral struggle against evil. His companionship is a defense against smugness. The intellectually discriminating atheist can be accepted as an ally in skeptically rejecting all the popular, half-baked stupidities named "god" that abound in our time and invited into conversations that explore what the best minds thought, and think, about God.

But there is one form of atheism that cannot be treated so charitably. Psalm 14 energetically attacks the one kind of atheism that the world is most tolerant of but of which it has most to fear—the people who say in their hearts, "There is no God." This is a quiet, unobtrusive atheism that never calls attention to itself. These people do not say with their mouths, "There is no God." To the contrary, with their mouths they say what everyone else says about God. They recite the Apostles' Creed and the Lord's Prayer along with the best of them. With their mouths they articulate impressive arguments for God's existence. With their mouths they denounce the godless. With their mouths they demand public prayers and official religion.

But in their hearts they say, "There is no God." Their atheism is never voiced and may not even be conscious, but it is lived—with a vengeance. When asked what they believe these atheists either subscribe to one of the religious fads of the day or assent to whatever the churches say should be believed about God. Philosopher-critic Alasdair McIntyre has formulated their creed: "That there is no God and that it is wise to pray to him from time to time."[3]

There is an undeniable exhilaration in saying "in the heart" there is no God: setting myself free from all dependency, being lord of all reality, finding that I can make people respond to my desires, acquiring skills that put me in control of situations. It is not unlike the exhilaration of leaving the intractable, hard-edged reality of land and swimming out into the ocean—an effortless, floating existence. I am bathed in the self and massaged by its currents. I have nothing to relate to but the self.

But for all its promise of immensity, the limitless horizons stretching out, the endless deeps beneath, it turns out to be a pretty small world. What can you, in fact, *do?* You can eat only with difficulty; you can converse merely fragmentarily; you can go no place. What kind of relations can you have with either things or persons? After awhile you get tired and need to get out. The self is not an environment in which you can live in any full, human sense.

We need God under our feet and God in our lungs. We need creator and creatures and community. God is the great continent of reality on which we live. If we deny him in practice by attempting to live in the ocean of the self, we are soon fatigued and require all kinds of artificial aids to keep us afloat—pieces of driftwood, life jackets. It is not our proper environment. We are forever getting our lungs full of water, getting rescued, receiving artificial respiration. Then we go out and start it all over again. Why don't we simply come out of the ocean of the self and stand on our own two feet on the dry land of the kingdom of God?

If, in fact, "there is no God," the self is both immediate and ultimate reality and we are stuck in it. But the self, like the womb (in itself an oceanic kind of existence), is something we must get out of if we are going to become a person.

People as Consumer Goods

There is more than the survival of the self at stake here; the survival of the world is also at stake, for these pleasant, respectable atheists of the heart endanger the world's health and sanity. They are moles in the world's mind, maggots in the world's body. The psalmist's fierce indictment is: "They eat up my people as they eat up bread." Cannibals! People are treated as consumer goods.

Heart-atheism becomes social oppression. If the self makes its own rules and satisfies its own compulsions, the social result is that the people around me become food—material that I can use to fulfill my needs. I no longer look on them as persons but as stuff that I can use to make life satisfactory.

One of the great lies of the age is that what I believe is nobody's business but my own, that what I do in the secrecy of my own heart is of no account to anyone else. But what I believe is everybody's business precisely because what goes on in my heart very soon shapes the way I act in society. If I am an atheist in my heart, making myself sovereign in place of God, and therefore arranging things in accordance with my appetites and needs and fantasies, I become a pirate in society. I relentlessly look for ways in which I can get what is there for my own uses with no regard for what anyone else gets. If I am an atheist in my heart, it is not long before I have become a cancer in the gut of the country.

G. K. Chesterton once said that if he were a landlord what he would most want to know about his tenants was not their employment, nor their income, but their beliefs, if there was any way he could truly find out. For it would be their beliefs that would determine their honesty, their relationships and their stewardship of the property. An adequate income is no proof against dishonesty. A reputable job is no guarantee against profligacy. Our beliefs are not off-the-cuff answers we give to an opinion survey; our beliefs are the deepest things about us. Our beliefs shape our behavior; therefore our beliefs are the most practical thing about us.

A Relational Word

Heart-atheism, which translates into self-righteousness, is not only evil, it is stupid: "Have they no knowledge, all the evildoers . . . ?" (v. 4). We think we know so much when we turn our backs on the mystery of God and acquire immense quantities of information on how to make the world work for us. But acquisition of information is not knowledge. Knowledge has to do with God, with his world, with his people. "God is with the generation of the righteous" (v. 5)—not the self-righteous, but those in right relationship with reality.

The biblical word *righteous* never refers to what we are in ourselves—no matter how good, how successful, how informed—but only to who we are in relationship with God. *Righteous* is a relational word, and the primary relation is with God.

Atheism is de-relational. It ungods God and makes the person of God an object that can be used or not used, denied or ignored, whichever I choose. At the same time that is going on, whether or not I intend it and whether or not I am aware of it, persons become unpersoned and thus objects to be used or not used, denied or ignored. When enough persons are treated this way, society becomes depersonalized and we no longer have a society but a factory outlet in which people are offered at discount.

The indictment continues: "You would confound the plans of the poor" (v. 6). The poor, throughout Scripture, are singled out for gracious visitation. There is a deep conviction, strongly voiced in both Old and New Testaments, that the poor and the wretched are the objects of God's particular interest.[4] When God selected a people to become the pioneer salvation community in history, he picked poor slaves in Egypt. When God became man, he was conceived in the womb of Mary in her poverty ("low estate," Lk 1:48) and lived as a poor man (2 Cor 8:9). When God created the church he gathered most of its population from the ranks of the poor (1 Cor 1:26-29).

Ronald Sider, surveying the sweep of biblical evidence in this regard, exclaims over the "astonishing and boundless" attention given to the poor.[5] Whenever the church has been vigorous and healthy it has given particular attention to the poor. Julian the Apostate, who hated Christians and did his best to discredit them, called them "godless Galileans" but was forced to admit that these so-called atheists "feed not only their poor but ours also."[6]

So why do the self-righteous, who know their Bibles as well as anyone, pick on the poor? Because the poor are a standing indictment against the grandiose foolishness of self-right-eousness. The poor present us with humanity stripped to the bare essentials, without utility, in whom we recognize ourselves nevertheless as kin. There is no cash value in the poor, yet the suffering, compassionate God confronts us in their faces. The poor is the person that is of no use to me, but who requires something of me.

But as sovereign of my life (by definition self-righteous— that is, righteous *without* relationship) I deny the relation-ship. How can I manage to fly in the face of so much evidence? By "confounding the plans of the poor," confusing the evidence, skewing the data. I denigrate the poor because they are lazy or denounce them because they are immoral or condescend to them because they are ignorant. How else could they be poor except through sloth or badness or stupidity?

The alternative to confounding the plans of the poor is to enter the company of the poor.[7] The poor, if we read Scripture carefully, are not a problem to be solved but people

to join. Charles Williams, who understood so well the ways
of the Holy Spirit in our history, observed that "the church
has never existed long anywhere without creating a demand
for a Revolution. 'The poor ye have always with you,' said
Christ, and wherever his tradition has gone we have been
made acutely aware of them."[8] A passion for social justice
germinates in this awareness.

There is a very close relation in Hebrew between the
words *poor ('aniyyim)* and *humble ('anawim)*. "Poor" desig-
nates a socioeconomic state; "humble," a moral-spiritual
condition. What they have in common is nonpossessiveness.
Whether by circumstance or by choice these people are not
in control. They either cannot or do not hold the reigns of
their destiny. Because they are out of control, they are able
to respond to and receive the gifts of God's sovereign bounty.

When Jesus began to teach his followers how to live by
faith, this is where he began. His words are given in two
versions: "blessed are the poor in spirit" *('anawim*—Mt 5:3);
"blessed are you poor" *('aniyyim*—Lk 6:20). Each is an analog
of the other: physical poverty is to the body what spiritual
poverty is to the soul. In a life characterized by God giving
himself and blessing us, we begin by not having. "All
disordered self-possession must be unlearned, if we are to be
made truly blessed. We must be weaned from ourselves and
our grip on ourselves. And the normal way in which we are
weaned is by being exposed to situations of mental, emotional and spiritual deprivation."[9]

No wonder the atheist of the heart is especially threatened
by the poor: in the presence of unself-righteousness, self-
righteousness is exposed for what it actually is, an unadmit-
ted but thoroughly practiced atheism. For as long as the poor
can be avoided or dismissed as inferior humanity, the
condition of *not having,* in which we realize that all that is
essential to our being comes from Another, can be avoided.
Our unvoiced atheism is undetected and unchallenged.

A Common Affliction

The alarming thing in this whole business is that it is so common.

> *The LORD looks down from heaven upon the children of men,*
>   *to see if there are any that act wisely,*
>   *that seek after God.*

Does he find anyone? No.

> *They have all gone astray, they are all alike corrupt;*
>   *there is none that does good,*
>   *no, not one.*

Paul quotes this in his great argument in Romans as he rips the cover off all human attempts to live in a self-justifying way (3:10-12). Jew and Greek, religious and irreligious, pious and pagan—we are all wrapped up in the self. We are all trying either to get along without God or to use God for our own purposes. In either case it is atheism: reducing God to nongod status so that I as my own god can either ignore him or command him to help me get what I want.

At least one of the reasons that this is so common is that it is so easy. Heart-atheism as opposed to head-atheism doesn't bother to deny God's existence with logical argument. That takes too much effort. Besides, it is not necessary. All that is necessary is to decapitalize him, demote him from God to god. I allow for his deity but restrict his jurisdiction to matters that don't impinge on my own sovereignty.

Heart-atheism, as opposed to moral-atheism, doesn't bother to protest God's existence with denunciatory speeches. That takes too much effort. Neither is it necessary. All that is necessary is to ignore the innocent suffering that calls his being into question. As long as I deal in terms that are economic and not moral, bureaucratic and not ethical, psychological and not spiritual, I don't have to deal with God.

Heart-atheism is the belief system (or unbelief system) of self-righteousness. It establishes the self at the center and arranges things, people, events and God around it in such ways that no matter what happens the self is right. *Vox egi vox dei* ("the voice of the I is the voice of God"). Everything is viewed and interpreted in relation to the sovereign self. This can often be managed with an extraordinary degree of success. There are always enough people around who act wickedly or stupidly so that blame for what is wrong with the world can plausibly be assigned to one of them without ever calling the sovereign self into question.

Lost Interest in God

Atheism, the attempt to be master of our fate and as many fates around us as we can decently manage, is not the bold swashbuckling affair of legend but a grim, tight-lipped business. These atheists are cramped, full of pretense, diminished beings. Either contemptuous or condescending toward the God whom they publically profess (their actual attitude toward the poor mirrors their inner attitude toward God), they depend on consumer goods or status positions or peer opinions—always something impersonal or abstract— to validate their sense of worth. With no inner life they require external paraphernalia, personalized things or depersonalized persons, to get a sense of self. Narcissism is the most recent term for this secret atheism of the heart. It typifies the character structure of a society that has lost interest in God.[10]

These people are fools. *Fool* is the Bible's most contemptuous term. The fool is the person who doesn't know what is going on in the cosmos. But he is not a person who is ignorant and searching, not a person who is lost and looking. The fool doesn't know that he doesn't know what is going on. He, in fact, thinks he knows it all, that he has it figured out, that he has the dope, that he knows the ropes. The fool lacks all the material for maintaining himself. He cannot devise plans that are worth anything. He must, finally, collapse. *Fool (nabal)* as a verb means "to collapse." Closely connected with this is the word for "corpse."[11] When the hot air has left the gaudy balloon, all that is visible is a limp bladder.

The opposite of *foolish* in Scripture is *wise*. *Wise* refers to skill in living. It does not mean, primarily, the person who knows the right answers to things, but one who has developed the right responses (relationships) to persons, to God. The wise understand how the world works; know about patience and love, listening and grace, adoration and beauty; know that other people are awesome creatures to be respected and befriended, especially the ones that I cannot get anything out of; know that the earth is a marvelously intricate gift to be cared for and enjoyed; know that God is an ever-present center, a never-diminishing reality, an all-encompassing love; and know that there is no living being that does not reach out gladly and responsively to him and the nation/kingdom/community in which he has placed us.

The wise know that there is only one cure for the fool. Prayer that is as passionate for the salvation of others as it is for myself: "O that deliverance for Israel would come out of Zion!" Prayer that is convinced that there is no wellness until everyone is restored to a place of blessing: "When the LORD restores the fortunes of his people." And prayer that sees the community as a place not of acquisition, but of celebration: "Jacob shall rejoice, Israel shall be glad" (v. 7).

9 Unself-Serving

God has taken his place in the divine council;
  in the midst of the gods he holds judgment:
"How long will you judge unjustly
  and show partiality to the wicked?
Give justice to the weak and the fatherless;
  maintain the right of the afflicted and the destitute.
Rescue the weak and the needy;
  deliver them from the hand of the wicked."

They have neither knowledge nor understanding,
  they walk about in darkness;
  all the foundations of the earth are shaken.

I say, "You are gods,
  sons of the Most High, all of you;
nevertheless, you shall die like men,
  and fall like any prince."

Arise, O God, judge the earth;
  for to thee belong all the nations!

Psalm 82

It is not right to acquiesce in the notion that a man's life is divided into the time he spends on his work and the time he spends in serving God. He must be able to serve God *in* his work, and the work itself must be accepted and respected as the medium of divine creation. . . . Every maker and worker is called to serve God *in* his profession or trade—not outside it.

Dorothy L. Sayers[1]

One of the most remarkable and daring claims of the Christian community, made early in the second century by Irenaeus and never repudiated or abandoned, was that God "became what we are that he might make us in the end what he is."[2] Two hundred years later Athanasius, in a fierce polemic waged against an enemy that he was convinced was at the jugular of our humanity, emboldened the claim: "He became man that we might become God."[3]

The claim is remarkable because these Christians accepted and lived in deliberate continuity with their Hebrew origins that insisted on an uncompromising monotheism: "God is God and there is no other." Out of the welter of gods and goddesses of the ancient world, Israel achieved a passionate and single-minded worship of one God. No exceptions were permitted: "The LORD your God is a jealous God."

The realization that God is one developed into a visionary international hope: because the nations and races were under a single sovereign and not champions for rival deities, world community and peace were possible (Is 2:1-5). The belief also provided the basis for the integration of the self. It prevented the multiplication of gods to correspond to the multiplication of desire, "god" a mere lever for prying loose from the exigencies of life whatever I cannot dislodge by my own strength.

Monotheism may seem to us a lumbering, obvious and bookish word, but to those believers it was a lightning-swift and shadow-piercing illumination: Live in integrated wholeness, unconflicted, unfragmented. Live in a world disarmed, undivided. It is remarkable that Christians who celebrated and defended this hard-won and much-attacked truth would countenance anything that even hinted of compromise.

To claim that there is anything potentially godlike in us is daring because the human desire to become gods, commonly described as pride, is ruinous. The first temptation narrated in Scripture is to "be like God" (Gen 3:5). If I become like God, I do not need God, being perfectly able to function as god on my own. Everyone with even ten minutes' experience in the human condition agrees that this is the root temptation. It insinuates itself into our lives in forms bold and subtle.

Knowing our propensity for playing God, our relentless ingenuity through self-deception or self-assertion to pretend to godlikeness, how could these wise and respected pastors, Irenaeus and Athanasius, dare to open the door even a crack for this temptation to enter? But they did, and they did with their eyes wide open to the dangers. They would not have denied that the statements brought immense risk. They took the risk because they were faced with even greater dangers than polytheism and pride, the danger of what came to be designated as Arianism.

Improbable Enemies

Arius was an improbable enemy. He was a Christian pastor in fourth-century Egypt and, from all reports, a decent enough person. Charles Williams describes him as "persuasive, virtuous, and ingenuous."[4] What he taught seemed plausible enough and innocent of any evil on first reading. He simply said that the actual life of God could not be shared or communicated. It stands to reason: God is so completely holy, so absolutely "other" that there is no way in which such holiness can be shared with humanity without compromising or tainting it, and he, of course, will not be compromised or tainted. Jesus, therefore, was not the expression of God in any direct or personal way; he was a creature, fashioned for the purpose of teaching us *about* God. God must necessarily keep his distance from us or he would cease to be God.

The relation between God and men and women, then, is a *teaching* relationship: didactic and moral. We are instructed, we are commanded, we are ordered around. But there is no shared experience of life, no love, no *communion*. The Arian world is one of absolute separation between God and humans. God is not a God who pours himself out in saving love but a benign tyrant who bullies people into goodness or, in other versions, a humorless pedant who drills pupils in their moral abc's. The Arian God was like the Roman Emperor: sublime, remote, despotic.

Athanasius, a young pastor in the same city, saw that Arius's arguments, honoring though they seemed to be of God, were demeaning to people. He sensed that there was some deep and inner connection between what we believe about God and the way we act every day, that we internalize what we conceive as God's action toward us and express it in social and political behavior.

If I believe that God cannot share himself in any personal or immediate way but only in impersonal and remote ways, I too will act that way. As a parent I will order my children around as servants instead of conversing with them as persons. I will treat my spouse as one who is there to meet my expectations instead of engaging in the difficult give and take of intimacy. As a worker I will attach more importance to the task than to the person doing the task. Each time I deny or suppress my capacity for personal relationship in favor of an impersonal status or function I lose a little of my own image-of-God humanity.

The way I think of God influences the way I think of myself and what I then become. The Arian way is to think of God as a creator but not a savior, an instructor but not a helper, a commander but not a lover. The effect of Arianism is to give us an omnipotent Technician instead of an eternal Father. The Technician makes and possesses and uses us as a potter makes and possesses and uses vessels. But if we are

clay pots, we do not have a father. We are orphans and there
is no gospel.[5]

Such a belief about God is radically de-relational, and the
great relational acts, love and prayer, gradually disappear.
For all its intellectual vigor and common-sense attractiveness,
Arianism was both scripturally and humanly abhorrent: a
religion without love and a religion without prayer.[6] It is
impossible to be human in any full sense without love and
prayer, without intimacy with each other and with God.
Athanasius insisted that neither is it possible to be God in
any scriptural sense without love and prayer. Jesus, who
loved and prayed among us, was not doing it to *show* us
something about God but was in actual fact being God with
us, sharing salvation in an intimacy and eternity beyond
Greek logic and Egyptian common sense. By being *with* us
and *in* us, a great transformation was set in operation: "he
became man that we might become God."

Unlikely as it seems, this argument between the two pastors
in Alexandria developed into the most significant political
event in the entire fourth century, raging across its decades,
provoking great synods and councils, setting off bloody
persecutions and demanding the full, if reluctant, attention
of six emperors. It is a striking historical documentation of
Charles Péguy's aphorism: "Everything begins in mysticism
and ends in politics."[7] The personal, inward intensities of
attending to God are concentrated into energies that expand
outward into community, government and culture. The
movement is not always so conspicuous, but it is always
happening.

Incarnation in Public

One prayer, which contributes to the remarkable and daring
claims to partake of the very nature of God and participate
in the very work of God, catapults Christians and Christian
communities time and again into the thick of world history.

It is Psalm 82. It puts monotheism at risk in order to draw
us into perceptions and responses that practice the incarnation in public.

The opening line is the praying precedent for Irenaeus
and Athanasius. With all their unremembered and unmen-
tioned kin, they ventured out of the security of their
sanctuaries—not without trepidation—into the streets as
"little Christs" (the original meaning of *Christian*).

God has taken his place in the divine council;
  in the midst of the gods he holds judgment.

No passage in the Psalms is as theologically demanding of
the translator. No literal translation satisfies. Literally the
sentence reads: "God *(elohim)* stands in the congregation of
God *(el)*; among gods *(elohim)* he judges." The translator's
difficulty is that the same word for God, *elohim,* is used twice
but with different meanings. The first meaning is clearly the
God of Israel, the Creator and judge of the universe. But
what is the second meaning? Using the context to interpret,
we see that it denotes the human judges of Israel, who have
been invested with a high, godlike work.[8] These "gods" are
accused of judging unfairly and are commanded to go out
and do it right (vv. 2-4). Their "godness" is reaffirmed in
verse 6 alongside their mortality in verse 7.

What we have, then, is not a theological definition but a
theological vision, a scenario of people at work at the jobs
assigned to them by God. God is presented as judge. But he
does not reserve the work exclusively to himself. He shares
it. This is surprising, for it is work that requires high
intelligence and stalwart virtue. Also, it is work that if done
badly reflects adversely on the Judge himself and calls into
serious question whether anyone is minding the store: "all
the foundations of the earth are shaken" (v. 5).

All those who have been given the work of judge are seen
in the vision gathered in convention, assembled around God
the Judge. The vision is spare and lean—no embellishments,

no anecdotes. *God* and *gods* occur five times (vv. 1, 6, 8); *judge* and *justice,* five times (vv. 2, 3, 8). The theme is clear: those who have been given God's work to do are called to give account.

The work of judges is to give justice, maintain the right, rescue and deliver. They have special responsibility to the weak, the fatherless, the afflicted, the destitute and the needy. These judges have not been doing their work. They have been judging by whim and prejudice. They have catered to the wealth and influence of the wicked. When a judge is wise and honest and fair, the results are apparent in the lives of those who appear before him. When a judge is foolish and dishonest and biased, the results are apparent in the lives of those who appear before him.

The evidence of history indicts the judges. How long will they continue to be unjust? They are called on the carpet: the judges are judged. They are not sovereign in their own work but are participants in God's work. That work, because it is derived from and delegated by God, makes them, functionally, gods. But it does not make them in themselves gods, for "you shall die like men" (v. 7).

These gods are not working as gods: they are betraying their calling in their actual work. They are attentive neither to its nature nor its purpose. "They have neither knowledge nor understanding, they walk about in darkness" (v. 5). What don't they know? What don't they understand? What don't they see? That in their *work* they are gods. They suppose that in *themselves* they are gods and they can therefore do what they please, but they are not and therefore cannot. If they do not do the work of gods in responsive obedience to God, they become nothing: "You are gods, sons of the Most High, all of you; nevertheless, you shall die like men, and fall like any prince" (vv. 6-7). If we take the godlike title and do not do the godlike work, we fool no one except ourselves. Death will unmask the illusion.

Hostile Questioning

This interpretation is corroborated by Jesus' use of Psalm 82. In the winter before his passion, he was hostilely questioned: "How long will you keep us in suspense? If you are the Christ, tell us plainly." Jesus said, "I and the Father are one." Stoning was the penalty for such monotheism-jeopardizing talk, and the Jews took up stones for the execution. Jesus asked, "I have shown you many good works from the Father; for which of these do you stone me?" The Jews countered, "It is not for a good work that we stone you but for blasphemy; because you, being a man, make yourself God." Jesus saved himself by quoting Psalm 82: "Is it not written in your law, 'I said, you are gods'? If he called them gods to whom the word of God came (and Scripture cannot be broken), do you say of him whom the Father consecrated and sent into the world, 'You are blaspheming,' because I said, 'I am the Son of God'?" (Jn 10:24-36).

Jesus allocates this word to himself, but he does not do so exclusively. "If he called them gods to whom the word of God came . . . " is the interpretive sentence. God by his word makes men and women "gods." By God's command the judges were gods, doing God's work. As in Genesis, so here. "He spoke, and it came to be" (Ps 33:9). Chaos became cosmos. Humans became judges participating in the divine administration of justice, and in that participation they became gods. "You are gods" is the startling ascription of the divine to humanly performed work. It sounds as blasphemous to us as it did to the Jews who challenged Jesus. But it is not blasphemy; it is incarnation.

Jesus uses the text in a way consistent with the psalm's meaning: his emphasis is not on his *being* but on his *working*, not on who he *is* but on what he *does*. In making this observation I do not overlook the strong emphasis throughout John's Gospel on the being of Jesus as also divine (the sequence of "I am" statements is comprehensive in that emphasis). But note that Psalm 82 is used to establish the *work* as a sign of participation in the divine: "The *works* that I do in my Father's name, *they* bear witness to me. . . . I have shown you many good *works* from the Father; for which of these do you stone me? . . . If I am not doing the *works* of my Father, then do not believe me . . . believe the *works*" (Jn 10:25, 32, 37, my italics).

Even though the important work of human judging was one work that we know Jesus quite deliberately excluded from his own practice ("Man, who made me a judge or divider over you?" Lk 12:14), he included himself within the scope of the psalm's reference. His own work was teaching, healing, preaching, visiting, praying and, most probably in his early years, carpentry. But Jesus understood the judges in the psalm as representative of all workers. His self-inclusion expands our frame of reference beyond the work of judges to all work: work as such is an assignment to participate in the divine work. No work is secular. No work is our own work. In no work are we "on our own."

We are godlike in our work because work originates in God and we are assigned to it by God. The intention of work is twofold: to continue the process of creation (Gen 2:15) and to counter the consequences of sin (Gen 3:17-19, 23). The original work of tending the garden was not abrogated by the Fall, but it was certainly complicated by the thorns and thistles.

The visionary gathering of judges in Psalm 82 engenders sequel visions: gatherings of teamsters, physicians, home-makers, lawyers, merchants, teachers, miners, foresters, farmers, sailors, pastors, soldiers, fishers, social workers, journalists, artists, longshoremen—as Whitmanesque a catalog of visions as we can manage. A vision is not a doctrine. The purpose of a vision is not to lay down clear lines of definition but to open up the horizons of the imagination to the expansive world of God's action. Visions are not cautious and careful but recklessly extravagant. We get glimpses of the awesomeness of our work, the holiness of our work, the meaning of our work. Work in its origin and intention is to further the blessings of creation and counter the effects of wickedness. Thus assembled, via the vision, my colleagues and I hear the question, "Is your work resulting in victims or in celebrants?"

Just as all work is designed to flow from God's work, so all work can also be deflected from it. Any work can be separated from its original goal so that it exploits or diminishes persons and things, societies and institutions. Work in its actual execution can use people and materials and ideas in self-serving ways so that the intent of creation is subverted and the ways of sin are increased. No work is exempt. Self-serving work is as possible in a church as in a factory. Exploitative work takes place as readily in the pulpit as in the hospital. Judges are corrupt. Presidents are crooks. Scientists are dishonest. Robert Louis Stevenson came upon a man on an Edinburgh street beating his dog. Stevenson intervened—grabbed the man by the lapels and pushed him up against the wall and rebuked him. The man whined, "It's my dog and I'll do what I want with it." Stevenson said, "It's not your dog; it's God's dog, and I'm here to protect it."

The vision prayed begins to sink in. The test of our work is not the profit we gain from it or the status we receive from it but its effects in creation. Are persons impoverished? Is the land diminished? Is society defrauded? Is the world less or more because of my work? We have become so accustomed to evaluating work in terms of productivity that we have little sense of its meaning in terms of creativity. We have for so long asked the questions of efficiency and profit that it does not even occur to us to ask the question of virtue. But Adam Smith is not canonical and Psalm 82 is. God gives us work— not to further our ambition or feather our nest but to deepen creation and sanctify society. No work can be reduced to

what we do for a living. All work is participation in the divine
work. God works and therefore we work, and in the work we
are gods. We direct energy, we fashion matter, we enter relationships, we "till and keep" earth and altar.

Psalm 82 becomes a boundary marker to warn against
prayer as pious withdrawal from the external world in order
to cultivate inner experience. Its vision shifts our attention
from the interior life to the whole range of exterior life in
our jobs and vocations. Gregory of Nyssa, one of the early
church fathers, did a masterful job of insisting that prayer to
God is impossible if it is confined in our heads or hearts:
there is nothing in prayer that can be distilled from life and
kept holy in a bottle. He directed attention to participation
not in what God *is*, but in what he *does*. "The man who shares
with the poor will have his share in the One Who became
poor for our sake. . . . We must so imitate the divine pity that
we may have the boldness to say to God, 'Copy Your servant,
Lord, Your poor and needy servant. I have forgiven, now You
forgive.' "[9] To become God, then, is to act as God acts—in
love, in poverty, in compassion—not merely a few evenings
a month and on weekends, but in our proper work. External-
izing is as much an act of prayer as internalizing.

Psalm 82 is cast in the form of a vision. In praying the
vision we see ourselves called to account before God. How
could we waste our lives so trivially in self-serving and thus
inflict such cruelty and waste on others? We see ourselves as
gods, not in boastful self-assertion but in awed realization:
we have life to spare, we have love left over, we have
compassion in excess, we have mercy in reserve. We are in
a position to do something for others, to exploit or to help,
to harm or to heal. We are not mere persons, getting on as
best we can, trying to stay out of the way of the big people
and pushing around the little people. We realize the
immense impoverishment both to ourselves and to the world
when our common work is routinely viewed as peripheral to

the life of faith. The vision recovers an original splendor and tests us against it in an act of judgment. Work can never again be what I am forced to do in order to get along as a human being. By means of the vision, returned to in prayer and repeatedly re-visioned, I recover my inclusion in the incredible statement, "You are gods."

From Seeing to Saying

But it is not quite all vision. At the very end there is a transition from seeing to saying. A cry breaks out,

Arise, O God, judge the earth;
for to thee belong all the nations!

"Arise, O God, judge. . . . " We think that when we pray we are getting God in on our operations. In fact he gets us in on his operations. Instead of giving God a job to do, we discover the job that he has given us to do, our failure in doing it, and how much we need his initiative to get the work going again in us and in all others. Invoking God to do his work, which I have come to realize is also my work, however bungled, I re-engage myself as participant in it, but now as unself-serving.

And then: "earth . . . nations." The vision has made it clear that we are not out to save our own skins but to care for the earth and the nations. The earth is as much a concern in prayer as the soul. The nations are as much a concern in prayer as the neighbor. The vision stirs and motivates us to pray with as much vehemence in regard to our earth and the nations as for our health and salvation. It is not a question of reducing the personal in order to concentrate on the political. The prayed vision expands our capacity so that we hold both in our field of vision and then utter both in our intercession.

Buckminster Fuller put forth the idea that the purpose of people on earth is to counteract the tide of entropy described in the Second Law of Thermodynamics. Physical things are falling apart at a terrific rate; people, on the other hand, put things together. People build bridges and cities and roads; they write music and novels and constitutions; they have ideas. That is why people are here. The universe *needs* somebody or something to keep it from falling apart. Fuller didn't include prayer in his work list, so I will supplement him: prayer remakes undoing.[10]

Prayed visions show the holiness of everyday human tasks. Intercessions restore disordered work and set it on its way again. Invocations interfere with the breakdown of cultures and systems and make *ora et labora* the motto that shapes our history.

10 Unself-Sufficient

When Israel went forth from Egypt,
  the house of Jacob from a people of strange language,
Judah became his sanctuary,
  Israel his dominion.

The sea looked and fled,
  Jordan turned back.
The mountains skipped like rams,
  the hills like lambs.

What ails you, O sea, that you flee?
  O Jordan, that you turn back?
O mountains, that you skip like rams?
  O hills, like lambs?

Tremble, O earth, at the presence of the LORD,
  at the presence of the God of Jacob,
who turns the rock into a pool of water,
  the flint into a spring of water.

Psalm 114

To make you or me, God must make half a universe. A man's body and a man's mind form a focus in which a world is concentrated, and drawn to a point.

Austin Farrer[1]

Blame for the ecological disorder of the twentieth century, it is widely held these days, must be placed at the door of the Christians. The accusation is supported by noting that Christians commonly put more store by eternal life than temporal life and that heaven counts for far more than earth in their value system: "This world is not my home, I'm just apassing through." Because their primary aim is to live eternally in the heavens, they have only leftover energies for taking care of the earth and give it short shrift.

This preference for heaven over earth is often accompanied by the conviction that this earth is destined for imminent destruction. Ill-fated as it is, it is difficult to work up enthusiasm for cleaning up rivers or preserving forests that are about to go up in the smoke of a doomsday conflagration anyway. With the earth far gone already in decay and corruption, a strip mine here and a radioactive waste dump there can hardly make things any worse than they are. It is a far better use of time to take care of matters of soul that will make them fit for habitation in the "new earth" that will descend from heaven after the judgment of this one.

The accusation is further documented by citing biblical texts that encourage Christians to exploit the earth. The Genesis text, "fill the earth and subdue it; and have dominion over the fish of the sea and over the birds of the air and over every living thing that moves upon the earth" (Gen 1:28), has been read by Christians, it is argued, as a license to do whatever they wished to earth, fish, birds and anything else that moves. *Subdue* means "put to use for my purposes." *Dominion* means "I am in charge." I can cut down the earth's forests without inquiring about consequences. I can slaughter its whales and egrets and buffalo at will. I can dump my waste in the rivers without a second thought. The earth and its resources are mine to use as I will; God said so.

The accusation develops by making comparisons with nonbiblical people. Primitive peoples have a very different relation to the earth: they are in awe of it and all the forces of nature—weather, seasons, wildlife, vegetation. There are great mysteries beyond understanding. These people live in both fear and reverence before the mountain, the river, the thunder. Pagan people, likewise, have a very different relation to the earth: they celebrate it and all the energies that move through it—the surge of life, the ecstasies of procreation, the shaping influence of sun and stars.

These people, the primitives and the pagans, know that there is something far greater than themselves in and under and over the earth. They learn the rituals and stories that keep them in harmony with it. But biblical peoples have a contempt for the earth. It is "beneath" them. They will enjoy and use it as they will, much as a master enjoys and uses a servant with little regard or even awareness that the servant has a dignity and a destiny that far surpasses the trivial task of making life convenient for the master. This attitude has made possible the widespread and unthinking ravaging of earth, sea and air. A primitive approach to nature could never have done this. A pagan approach to nature would never have allowed this. A biblical approach to nature provided the attitudes and rationalizations that made it possible.[2]

Nature in Tatters
That is the accusation. Is it true?

Hardly. The accusation is fashioned out of a shameful ignorance of the biblical mind and an inexcusable ignorance of modern history. That men and women in this century have raped the earth is true enough. At no time in human history has there been anything remotely approaching it. The French philosopher Maurice Merleau-Ponty summed up the results of our modern willfulness with grim brevity: "Nature is in tatters."[3]

But responsibility for this profanation of the earth cannot credibly be assigned to the biblical mind. It is true that the biblical revelation, in contrast to primitive and pagan religions, did not see nature as divine and therefore to be worshiped. It viewed it as *creation:* brought into existence by the word of God and thus a revelation of goodness and blessedness. Humans are not subservient to the natural world (the view of pagans and primitives); therefore, they are no longer in terror of it or in ecstasy because of it. But neither are we above it in any way that allows us to look down on it carelessly or condescendingly.

As the most fully developed of the creatures, as creatures that "in the image of God" can volitionally participate in the ways of God, we have immense responsibilities to "cultivate and take care of" the garden (Gen 2:15 JB) and to be "stewards of the mysteries" (1 Cor 4:1). Creation is not an alien to be treated with hostility, superstition or indifference; it is made by the same Creator who made man and woman, who are therefore in kinship with all the elements of creation. Appreciative responsibility and grateful mutuality are the attitudes engendered by the biblical texts.

Contempt for the earth is not ancient but modern, not biblical but secular. The revolution in human thinking and action that was introduced by the age of the so-called Enlightenment is, more than anything else, responsible for it. In that intellectual-spiritual movement the human took charge of all things, the self and the world. World views were secularized so that there was no longer a God of love and justice to answer to, only a humanity of ambition and self-interest to give commands. "Glory to man in the highest and on earth a higher standard of living for all" was the theme hymn. Earth is here for our *use* not for our *care.* Technological developments provide increasingly powerful means to impose human will on the environment at the same time that spiritual understandings, which restrain pride and cultivate humility, diminish.

As the "image of God" as the controlling metaphor for understanding our place in the universe fades and the myth of self-sufficiency replaces it, fewer and fewer people ask the question, "What is the purpose of God in creation?" They ask instead, "How can I use creation to fulfill my purposes?" Purposes are not evaluated against God's purposes. It is simply assumed that what is good for the human is good for everything.

Torn out of the context of divinely purposed creation, human willfulness makes its own decisions without submitting them to a higher court (for most people there is no higher court). No longer are forests places where thoughtful people stroll, losing themselves in the rapture of quietness, praying in gratitude to the Maker; they are invaded by technicians calculating how many bulldozers are needed to level it for a new subdivision. The wise passiveness of the creature at home with other creatures is exchanged for the nervous clutch of the technologist at the controls of a machine.[4] Not always, of course, and not by everyone. There are still people who are sensitive to human values and moral realities and who carefully use technology to the glory of God. But they are a remnant people.

In the wake of the devastation that is apparent on all sides in this deification of the greedy, gluttonous, power-hungry, vain and impulsive will, and in light of the accusation that the biblical mind is responsible for it, concerned people are going to primitive or pagan models for inspiration and direction. Many Christians have been stampeded into joining them. We will do far better if we do what we do best: pray. We have a centuries-deep tradition of gathering the elements of the environment into acts of prayer, which puts us both in tune with the creation and at the service of the Creator

so that his continuing work becomes our work too. Praying
after the manner of certain psalms puts us in a place of
intercession that develops actions that unself America in
relation to the earth. Psalm 114 is one place to begin.

Antiprayer
The most striking thing about Psalm 114 is its imagery: the
sea fleeing and Jordan running away, the mountains and
hills skipping like rams and lambs, the rock and flint gushing
streams of water. This is prayer that is immersed in an
awareness of the creation, at home in the earth, sensitive to
the life of the nonhuman aspects of the environment.

On second look, it turns out that the prayer is not about
nature but about history: an event—the exodus from Egypt—
is being prayed. On further examination we find that there
are, in fact, no "nature" psalms in Scripture, that is, psalms
about or addressed to nature.

There are psalms in which our experience with and
knowledge of sky and sea, animals and birds are used in the
vocabulary of prayer, but it is always something about God,
not nature, that is being prayed. Psalmists praise his act of
creation (33); express awe at his incredible condescension
in including humans in a responsible position (8); juxtapose
the twin glories of sky and law in revealing God's design (19);
marvel at the scheme of providence that is so impressively
worked out in the intricate interrelations of light, wind,
cloud, oceans, springs, birds, fish, storks, badgers, people at
work and people at praise (104). But their psalms are never
about nature; always they are about God.

The biblical poets did not go in for nature appreciation;
in fact, they were in vehement opposition to it. Their
opposition was quite deliberate, for the Hebrews lived in a
world where all their neighbors prayed to nature. The most
prominent aspects of nature are fecundity and destruction:
the hidden processes of birth in earth and womb on the one

hand and, on the other hand, the terrible forces of volcano, earthquake and storm that are quite beyond any prediction or control. The Canaanites (and all the surrounding nations in the extrabiblical world were much the same) were in awe of and prayed to this divinity that was beyond them. It is easy to see why they did it, for in unguarded moments we do it still. It is not easy to account for why the Hebrews did not.

The created world around us is wondrous. Any moment that we attend to it, feelings and thoughts are roused that take us out of ourselves, feelings and thoughts that seem very much like prayer. These are so spontaneous and uncontrived, so authentic and unpretentious, that there is little doubt that we are in some deep communion with a reality beyond us, with gods—or God. Compared to our experience in the scheduled hours of worship at established places of prayer, these always seem more genuine, which accounts perhaps for the frequently voiced preference for sunsets on the beach over eighteenth-century hymns in chapel.

But when we return to such natural settings in order to recover such feelings, what ordinarily happens is that we become more attentive to our feelings than to God. We have crossed a line. We are not praying but "using" nature to produce religious feelings. We enter into the mysterious rhythms of the seasons; we give ourselves to the ecstasies of weather; we open ourselves to the influence of sun and planets.

In itself, there is nothing particularly wrong with this and much that is right. What is wrong is when it develops into a systematic manipulation and exploitation of nature. In the course of submitting to natural forces and absorbing the energies of divine nature, there comes a point at which one wonders if the influence might not be reversed so that the powers that have been received into the self might somehow now be redirected to influence nature. It sounds plausible. The experiment is engaged. Another line is crossed. We are using creation to alter creation, turning creation against itself.

The practice is common enough to get a fancy name: *homeopathy*, cultivating the feelings/rhythms/actions of divine nature so that divine nature will come under my influence. Nature religion operates on the principle that there is something divine in mountains and rivers, in moon, in sun and stars, in seasons and weather. By "getting into" nature one gets into the divine, participates in the fertility, enlists on the victorious side, experiences immortal ecstasies. There are divine forces in creation that can be offended or appeased. By engaging in the proper rituals and with a little bit of luck, we can manipulate nature for selfish benefit.

This is the origin of the antiprayer called magic. Prayer is willingness practiced before God; magic is willfulness exercised on nature. Magic is the skilled use of natural means to manipulate the supernatural (whether God or devil) in order to bend the natural to respond to my will. The magician is expert in using the lore of herbs, the movements of planets, the incantation of sounds, the concoction of potions, the making of diagrams (all from the realm of nature) in order to impose his or her will on nature. In the days of the psalmists this religion was Baalism.[5] Today this religion surfaces in one form of Faustian technology or another (*using* nature to orchestrate a lust for feelings, *using* nature to satisfy a lust for power, and so forth).

The comic account in 1 Kings 18, in which the priests of Baal gashed themselves with stones so that their blood flowed in an attempt to influence the skies into pouring rain, is the most famous biblical story of homeopathy. If they could only make the vital, life-carrying liquid from their bodies flow in sufficient quantity, surely the life-carrying liquid from the sky-god Baal would also flow. Elijah, by contrast, does not *do* anything. In prayer we do not act, God does. In prayer we do not develop a technology that sets the

gears and pulleys of miracle in motion, we participate in
God's action: "not my will but yours."

Modern technologists are successors to pagan magicians.
The means have changed but the spirit is the same: metal
machines and psychological methods have replaced magic
potions, but the intent is still to work my will on the environment, regardless. God is not in on it, or he is in on it only
insofar as he can be used in ways that accommodate the
lordly self.

The Scene of God's Action

Psalm 114, meanwhile, holds the focus on prayer, not magic.
It deals with the way God is acting with nature as his
accomplice. There is nothing here of how we can manipulate
nature in order to shape history to our convenience. The
earth is not here for us to use; the earth is the scene of God's
action. In pride we approach nature to use it; in prayer the
psalmist directs us to join it in praise and celebration of God's
salvation.

When Israel went forth from Egypt,
   the house of Jacob from a people of strange language,
Judah became his sanctuary,
   Israel his dominion.

The most unobtrusive words in these lines, the pronouns, are
the very ones that turn out to be most important: *his*
sanctuary, *his* dominion; that is, *God's* sanctuary, *God's*
dominion. The formative experience for Israel's identity, the
exodus, is not arrogantly held up as a nationalist banner
behind which they can march, boasting of their superiority.
What is expressed instead is unpretentious submission to
God's gracious rule. Geography (Judah) becomes liturgy
(sanctuary). A piece of land in the ancient East becomes an
arena in which the divine action is played out. The two ways
that we commonly use to locate ourselves in reality (where
we are and what we see) are subsumed into things both

larger and more intimate, God's presence and God's action. History and geography are gathered into worship.

The biblical, praying mind does not reduce place to a matter of geology, mapping and analyzing, nor to a matter of economics, assigning ownership, but views it in terms of God's presence and action in our environment. The biblical, praying mind does not abstract God from nature. Rocks and rivers, whales and elephants are participating elements in salvation. God is not understood by means of nature but nature by means of God. Nature is not pronounced divine and so made to bear more freight than she can hold so that at one moment, gripped by fearful superstitions, we cower before her; at another, infatuated with mental illusions, we coyly court her. Nor is God reduced to nature so that we can "handle" him, convinced that if we only learn the right technique we can use him for our purposes.

Something more like a sacrament is realized: the exodus from Egypt and the entrance into Canaan are the means that God used to make himself known and become present to his people. He did not do this apart from geographically locatable history. The land and its scenery are not means that the people use to influence God but the material structure of his action among them. They pray to *him*, not to a "divine" stone. They pray to *him*, not to a petrified god.

The difference between a sacrament and an idol (or an amulet, incantation, ritual or figurine) is that a sacrament is what God uses to give and an idol is what we use to get. The material is involved in either case, but before the sacrament we are willing and before the idol we are willful. Sacraments are, therefore, everyday material (rivers and lambs; water, bread, wine), because God uses whatever is commonly at hand to share himself with us. Idols, in contrast, are exceptional material—precious metals fashioned into impressive shapes, unusual objects like meteorites that will supplement our willfulness and add potency to our aspirations after lordship. When, though, we attend sacramentally to God, he uses our awareness to throw a widening light across the environment that shows Egypt and Palestine (and America) as material places where God acts redemptively.

A Way of Victory

The way in which this sacramental sense shapes our relation to our environment is expressed in the middle lines of the prayer.

The sea looked and fled,
  Jordan turned back.
The mountains skipped like rams,
  the hills like lambs.

At one level this is simply a colorful account of the exodus: "The sea looked and fled." In the more sober language of prose, this is the story of Israel. Fleeing from the Egyptians and then blocked at the waters of the Red Sea, the people walked through on dry land after Moses struck the waters with his staff and the waters parted. God "provided a way of escape." "Jordan turned back" remembers Israel's being prevented from entering the Promised Land at the conclusion of her forty years' wilderness trek by the formidable Jordan River. Then Joshua struck the waters with his staff, the river parted, and the people marched through and began their conquest of the land. God provided a way of victory. In the prose of the book of Exodus, "the mountains skipped like rams, the hills like lambs" is the story of the long wait of the people at the base of Sinai in awe before the volcanic-rumbling and earthquake-shaken mountain while Moses was on the heights receiving the law.

Why not say it plainly? For one thing, God's action and presence among us is so beyond our comprehension that sober description and accurate definition are no longer functional. The levels of reality here are so beyond us that they invite extravagance of language. But the language, though extravagant, is not exaggerated. All language is inadequate and falls short. The picture of the Red Sea as a fleeing jackal, the Jordan as a cowardly sentinel forsaking his post, the transformation of Sinai to frolicking rams and lambs is not, of course, a journalistic account of what happened, but neither is it the fabrication of an unhinged imagination. It is people at prayer witnessing salvation. The somersaulting of what everyone had assumed to be the limitations of reality (the Red Sea and the Jordan River) and the unexpected outpouring of energy where there was nothing but a huge, dead, granite outcropping in the dead desert (Sinai) called for the new use of old words.

Something else is involved, something even more significant. In prayer we acquire what Wallace Stevens called "a motive for metaphor." We see far more than discrete *things*, we perceive everything in dynamic tension and relationship with everything else. The raw stuff of the world is not matter but energy. How do we express this interconnected vitality? We use metaphor.

A metaphor is a word that bears a meaning beyond its naming function; the "beyond" extends and brightens our comprehension rather than confusing it. Just as the language of ecology demonstrates the interconnectedness of all *things* (air, water, soil, persons, birds, and so forth), the language of imagination and metaphor demonstrates the interconnectedness of all *words*. The historical word *(exodus)*, the geological word *(hills)* and the animal word *(ram)* all have to do with every other word.

Meanings interconnect. Nothing can be understood in isolation, pinned down under a microscope; no *word* can be understood by merely locating it in a dictionary. From the first moment we speak, we are drawn into the total web of all language that has ever been spoken. One word draws us into surprising relationships with another, and then another, and then another. That is why prayer is so fond of words used imaginatively: metaphor, simile, metonymy, hyperbole. Prayer is not using language to construct a vocabulary list of what is *there* but to connect and involve us in an associative *syntax* in which everything is in movement, finding its place in relation to the word that God speaks.

Wendell Berry says it well: "The earth is not dead, like the concept of property, but is as vividly and intricately alive as a man or a woman and . . . there is a delicate interdependence between its life and our own."[6] And so the imaginative statement "the mountains skip like rams" is not mere illustration to portray the exuberance of the Sinai revelation; it is a penetrating realization that the earth itself responds to and participates in the revelation. Paul used a different, though just as striking, image for the action: "We know that the whole creation has been groaning in travail together until now; and not only the creation, but we ourselves" (Rom 8:22-23). Metaphor and simile do not explain; they draw us away from being outsiders into being insiders, involved with all reality spoken into being by God's word.

Language is debased when it uses metaphor as decoration to cover scrawny thoughts, putting lace cuffs on bare-wristed prose. In actual fact, imaginative language is not what we learn to use after we have mastered the rudiments of plain speech. Imaginative language is prior to descriptive language. As infants, we all started out as poets, using words to praise and exclaim and comment. The most original and accurate speech is metaphorical—words that discover an underlying unity in which we, often with surprise, perceive that we fit, that we belong.

"Robert Frost reminds us that 'Metaphor is taking one thing for another.' In this sense, all language is metaphorical, for it insistently connects one thing with another. A word, any word, perpetually sends out tentacles of connectedness everywhere."[7] We are not objects in an environment, we are residents in a home. "World" is not impersonal stuff to study and use; it is interpenetrated by spirit—God's Spirit, my spirit. We are a part of what we know.

Now we realize that prayer and poetry are the closest of kin. Every word draws us closer to where words come from: the creative word that makes mountains and rams, hills and lambs, Israel and Judah, Jacob and Christ, me and you. In poetry we say it; in prayer we become what we say as we encounter the One who originates all saying.

Tremble, O Earth

The personal that is at the heart of the natural is expressed in the final stanza.

> *Tremble, O earth, at the presence of the LORD,*
> *at the presence of the God of Jacob,*
> *who turns the rock into a pool of water,*
> *the flint into a spring of water.*

Earth is comprehensive here: Egypt, Israel, Judah, sea, Jordan, mountains, hills. At the deepest level we are not divided into "animal, vegetable, mineral." Together, we are before the presence of God. God's presence is not Sinai's thunder, not Jordan's billows, not Egypt's chariots. It is that before which we are in awe.

Tremble here reaches for the transcendental: awed respect, reverent humility. Promethean man trembles before neither earth nor altar; he takes charge. Technological man trembles before neither forest nor angel host; he operates his slide rule unemotionally with steady hands. People at prayer tremble, along with the whole creation that "waits with eager longing" (Rom 8:19) and in hopeful adoration before the mystery of creation and redemption in which "in everything God works for good" (Rom 8:28).

Paul attempted to trace the process with the ponderous words *predestination, justification, glorification.* His attempt has been useful in many ways, but I doubt whether his theological thinking gets us much beyond "the outskirts of his ways."

Later he returned to the more fundamental language of prayer: "O the depths of the riches and wisdom and knowledge of God! How unsearchable are his judgments and how inscrutable his ways!" (Rom 11:33). Here we find ourselves closer to the reality and in the presence of God's action, rather than just thinking about it.

Trembling is not, as outsiders so often think, being scared in the presence of God. It is something more like a holy playfulness, like faith frolicking. "Nature" is commonly viewed as a vast mathematical structure of cause and effect, the skies and oceans governed by rod-of-iron rules. Anyone who dares defy them is "broken in pieces like a potter's vessel." The iron rod of gravity, for instance, shatters my leg as I fall out of a tree. The iron rule of thermodynamics burns my finger as I retrieve my fork from the fire.

Prayer is not defiant or dismissive of these necessities but instead knows that there is more than necessity in the environment; there is also freedom. The moment we understand that, playfulness is born. Prayer that enters into relationship with earth and sky, sea and mountain, plays. It skips and dances. We do not live in an ironclad universe of cause and effect. In the presence of the God of Jacob there is life that is beyond prediction. There is freedom to change, to become more than we were in the presence of the God who "turns the rock into a pool of water, the flint into a spring of water."

Miracles are not interruptions of laws, which must then either be denied by worried intellectuals or defended by anxious apologists; they are expressions of freedom enjoyed by the children of a wise and exuberant Father. We do not solve these things with rigorous exegesis of the biblical text or with controlled experiments in a laboratory; we *pray* them and in praying enter into dimensions of personal freedom in the universe. At some level (probably beyond the level of academic comprehension, although not necessarily; the writings of the "new physics" are unexpectedly illuminative of these truths), we are in a dance. In it, necessity and freedom are synchronized and responsive to each other, each dependent on the other, alive and personal.

Our True Home

We do not begin life on our own. We do not finish it on our own. Life, especially when we experience by faith the complex interplay of creation and salvation, is not fashioned out of our own genetic lumber and cultural warehouses. It is not hammered together with the planks and nails of our thoughts and dreams, our feelings and fancies. We are not self-sufficient. We enter a world that is created by God, that already has a rich history and is crowded with committed participants—a world of animals and mountains, of politics and religion; a world where people build houses and raise children, where volcanos erupt lava and rivers flow to the sea; a world in which, however carefully we observe and watch and study it, surprising things keep on taking place (like rocks turning into pools of water). We keep on being surprised because we are in on something beyond our management, something over our heads.

In prayer we realize and practice our part in this intricate involvement with absolutely everything that is, no matter how remote it seems to us or how indifferent we are to it. This prayer is not an emotional or aesthetic sideline that we indulge in after our real work is done; it is the connective tissue of our far-flung existence. The world of creation interpenetrates the world of redemption. The world of redemption interpenetrates the world of creation. The extravagantly orchestrated skies and the exuberantly fashioned earth are not background to provide a little beauty on the periphery of the godlike ego; they are the large beauty in which we find our true home, room in which to live the cross and Christ expansively, openhearted in praise.

11 Unself-Love

My heart overflows with a goodly theme;
I address my verses to the king;
my tongue is like the pen of a ready scribe.

You are the fairest of the sons of men;
grace is poured upon your lips;
therefore God has blessed you for ever.
Gird your sword upon your thigh, O mighty one,
in your glory and majesty!

In your majesty ride forth victoriously
for the cause of the truth and to defend the right;
let your right hand teach you dread deeds!
Your arrows are sharp
in the heart of the king's enemies;
the peoples fall under you.

Your divine throne endures for ever and ever.
Your royal scepter is a scepter of equity;
you love righteousness and hate wickedness.
Therefore God, your God, has anointed you
with the oil of gladness above your fellows;
your robes are all fragrant with myrrh and aloes and cassia.
From ivory palaces stringed instruments make you glad;
daughters of kings are among your ladies of honor;
at your right hand stands the queen in gold of Ophir.

Hear, O daughter, consider, and incline your ear;
  forget your people and your father's house;
  and the king will desire your beauty.
Since he is your lord, bow to him;
  the people of Tyre will sue your favor with gifts,
  the richest of the people with all kinds of wealth.

The princess is decked in her chamber with gold-woven robes;
  in many-colored robes she is led to the king,
  with her virgin companions, her escort, in her train.
With joy and gladness they are led along
  as they enter the palace of the king.

Instead of your fathers shall be your sons;
  you will make them princes in all the earth.
I will cause your name to be celebrated in all generations;
  therefore the peoples will praise you for ever and ever.

Psalm 45

**So often when we say "I love you" we say it with a huge "I"
and a small "you." We use love as a conjunction instead of it
being a verb implying action.**

Anthony Bloom[1]

P rayer is the action that gets us in touch with and develops the most comprehensive relationships—self, God, community, creation, government, culture. We are born into a web of relationships and continue in it throughout our lifetimes. But we often don't feel like it. We feel isolated, cut off, fragmented, out of touch. We do not tolerate such isolation very well and move out to overcome it: we call up a neighbor, join a club, write a letter, get married. The disparate attempts accumulate. The self is less isolated. Society is less fragmented. The facts add up. But if we do not pray, they do not add up to enough: in prayer and only in prayer are we able to enter the complexity and depth of the dynamic and interrelated whole. A failure to pray is not a harmless omission; it is a positive violation of both the self and the society.

If we deny our relationships, we are pirates in society, taking but not giving. The world of things and people is viewed as loot to plunder. If we are ignorant of our relationships, we are parasites, passively leeching nutrients from the body politic and making only a negative contribution to the lives of others. Prayer is the source-action that prevents, on the one hand, our defection as pirates and, on the other hand, our deformation into parasites.

This is never more apparent than in the act of love. Being in love is the best way to live as an individual; being in love is the best way to live as a citizen. Love brings the self to the highest pitch; love brings society to its most mature expression. Love is the one act in which the public and the personal coinhere most dramatically, where unnoticed relationships quite beyond calculation blossom into view in a welcoming and attractive way. In the act of love national interest and individual interest are pursued simultaneously.

But love is also the one act in which we appear at our

worst. If love is the field of our most exquisite achievements, it is also the stage for our most embarrassing pratfalls. Love is the highest act of which humans are capable; it is also the source of our greatest miseries. Ecstasies develop out of love, but the same dynamics often misfire into violence. More murders are committed in the bedrooms of America than in any other location.

The inner connection between the personal and the public in all matters of love is given outward form in the wedding. There is nothing more personal than a wedding, two persons freely coming together and giving themselves to the joys of intimacy. There is also nothing more public: intimacies involve responsibilities, so a document from the state is required, a public official is assigned to the ceremony, witnesses from the community attest to the action, and the event is recorded in a government register. The wedding affirms the wholeness in love between two persons; it also declares that the health of society is at stake. The wedding gathers the personal and the public into a single act. Weddings most commonly take place, even when the people themselves do not pray, in the place of prayer.

And yet we are slow to believe that love is an appropriate political act. "A couple who make a good marriage," writes Wendell Berry, "and raise healthy, morally competent children, are serving the world's future more directly and surely than any political leader, though they never utter a public word."[2] The wedding, set at the boundary of the personal and the public, continues to give us fresh opportunities for new beginnings in love that embrace both individual and society. Our slowness to explore these dimensions is avoidance. We are wrapped up in self-love. We venture in brief moments of romantic infatuation to include another, but we are reluctant to go beyond spouse, or child, or friend. Neighbors, bosses, groups, causes, bureaucracies, nations, peoples, races—these are dealt with under other labels such as precedent, custom, protocol, national interest, economic feasibility.

Sacred to Secular

Psalm 45 is a wedding song. As such it integrates the personal and the public in the celebrative way that is characteristic of weddings. It is not, strictly speaking, a prayer but a song addressed to bride and groom in the presence of God. Yet in the course of centuries of inclusion in the worship of temple, synagogue and church, it has in fact become prayer, an especially powerful prayer in the unselfing of love.

The transition from the secular to the sacred is fairly common in prayer. Words that are arranged to deal with everyday expediencies become involved in a larger reality and in this larger context are transformed into prayer. The dinner-table phrase "pass the bread" is the experiential basis for "give us this day our daily bread." A wedding song, composed and sung for an unnamed bride and groom in ancient Israel, is put into a prayer book, the Psalms, and directs the unselfing of love in the prayers of contemporary Americans.

My heart overflows with a goodly theme;
I address my verses to the king; . . .
at your right hand stands the queen in gold of Ophir.

The public quality of this wedding is accentuated by naming the bride and groom "king" and "queen" (vv. 1 and 9). A state wedding! The marriage of a Hebrew king and his Tyrian queen is celebrated in this festive song. Royal weddings are political events. But they are no less romantic unions. In our democratic society where the only royal weddings we see are telecast from Great Britain, which still has a few vestiges of monarchy, the romantic side of the wedding is all that we pay attention to. But in fact every wedding is a state wedding, authorized and regulated by legislation.

In the midst of the candles and gowns, stirring songs and

fervent vows, embraces and kisses, there is also a license, sometimes quite unceremoniously crumpled in someone's pocket or purse. Wedding celebrants in many cultures dress the bride and groom as king and queen with crown and tiara, scepter and train. The formal dress emphasizes the importance of the partners to each other, but it also recognizes the continuing impact of their marriage in society even though they will live out their years of marriage in clothing more suitable for factory and market and farm.

Love in its mature form is both personal and public and is displayed as such in the wedding ceremony. But we do not often see it develop an inclusive wholeness. The postwedding withdrawals of love are more common than its ventures. The immaturities of love are more in evidence than its perfections. But love that withdraws from the public into the private is irresponsible to the nation. It cultivates private delight and abandons community responsibility.

The withdrawal, however, can go the other direction too: love that withdraws from the personal to the public is irresponsible to family and friends. Leo Tolstoy had the entire world's attention for a few years as he proclaimed the principle of love as public policy, the way to bring nations into peace and wholeness. But his own children complained, "Papa loves the world but he kicks his own children around like dogs."[3]

Of all the hyphenations of the self, self-love is the most destructive. Love is our primary relational mode, just as it is God's in whose image we are made. If we use love nonrelationally, that is, selfishly, it is an abomination that corrupts society and ruins the self.[4] But its destructiveness is often undetected for long stretches because it goes under the appealing name of "love." Luther analyzed sin as the person *incurvatus in se,* curved in on the self. When sin causes love to curve in on itself it produces its most grotesque work. The area in which this grotesque work is most on display is in marriage. The psalm, by placing a romantic wedding in a political setting, provides a large stage on which to direct the mature development of love and protect against its debasement.

No protestation of love, no matter how public and how passionate, is a guarantee against slipping back into mere love of self. This poem-become-prayer, Psalm 45, takes two basic elements of love and directs them in ways that guard against the distortions of self-love and develops them into the beauties of mature love. The first element, addressed to the king-groom, is *adoration;* the second, addressed to the queen-bride, is *detachment*. Prayed adoration and detachment are our best personal cures for self-love. They are also of great moment in our political life.

Is Love Blind?

You are the fairest of the sons of men;
grace is poured upon your lips;
therefore God has blessed you for ever.
Gird your sword upon your thigh, O mighty one,
in your glory and majesty!

In your majesty ride forth victoriously
for the cause of truth and to defend the right;
let your right hand teach you dread deeds!
Your arrows are sharp
in the heart of the king's enemies;
the peoples fall under you.

Your divine throne endures for ever and ever.
Your royal scepter is a scepter of equity;
you love righteousness and hate wickedness.
Therefore God, your God, has anointed you
with the oil of gladness above your fellows;
your robes are all fragrant with myrrh and aloes and cassia.

From ivory palaces stringed instruments make you glad;
daughters of kings are among your ladies of honor;
at your right hand stands the queen in gold of Ophir.

This first half of the psalm (vv. 2-9) is unchecked and cascading adoration, an exuberant and extravagant admiration. The groom is perceived as handsome ("fairest of the sons of men"), well spoken ("grace is poured upon your lips"), heroic ("your arrows are sharp in the heart of the king's enemies"), good ("you love righteousness and hate wickedness"), glad ("from ivory palaces stringed instruments make you glad") and fortunate in love ("at your right hand stands the queen in gold of Ophir").

If I, deeply in love with another, begin describing with passionate appreciation what has been unnoticed or ignored by everyone else for years, some people around me are sure to dismiss me, "Love is blind." They mean that love diminishes my capacity to see what is actually there so that fantasy, tailor-made to fit my desires, can be projected on another and thus make him or her acceptable as a lover. The cynical follow-up is that if this did not happen, if I saw the other truly, I would never get involved. Why? Because everyone is, in fact, quite unlovely, either visibly or invisibly, or, in some particularly unfortunate cases, both. Love doesn't see truth but creates illusions and incapacitates us for dealing with the hard-edged realities of life.

But the popular saying, as popular sayings so often are, is wrong. It is hate that is blind. It is habit, condescension, cynicism that are blind. Love opens eyes. Love enables the eyes to see what has been there all along but was overlooked in haste or indifference. Love corrects astigmatism so that what was distorted in selfishness is now perceived accurately and appreciatively. Love cures shortsightedness so that the blur of the distant other is now in wondrous focus. Love cures farsightedness so that opportunities for intimacy are no longer blurred threats but blessed invitations. Love looks at the one who had no "form or comeliness that we should look at him, and no beauty that we should desire him" and sees there the "fairest of the sons of men . . . anointed with the oil of gladness above your fellows."

If we could see the other as he is, as she is, there is no one we would not see as "fairest . . . all fragrant with myrrh and aloes and cassia." Love penetrates the defenses that have been built up to protect against rejection and scorn and belittlement, and it sees life created by God for love. When we look through eyes diseased by self-love, we see neither beauty nor virtue. We stumble in a blurred, unfocused, misshapen world and complain that it is ugly or threatening or boring.

Self-love twists the spontaneities of admiration into calculations of envy. Everything attractive and desirable is given a price tag. Instead of dancing and exclaiming in a world of wonders, we stalk the aisles and comparative shop, asking, "How much?" The impulses in us that are designed to mature into adoring love are perverted into scheming acquisition. We live, consequently, in a society in which transactions, both material and personal, are based on envy. Advertising promotes consumption as a way of life, developing unappeasable appetites not only for goods but also for new experiences and personal fulfillment. Society is expected to provide both things and people in endless supply to satisfy these envy-goaded appetites. Envy and its attendant anxieties replace adoration with its inventive praises as the dominant mood of self-love.

Nothing less than prayer is personal and powerful enough to counter these omnipresent, envy-inciting stimuli and redirect toward the adoration of God and others the enormous energies of love that curve in on the self. Following the lead of Hebrews 1:9, Christians use Psalm 45 to develop adoration of Christ, in whom we encounter the human and the divine at one and the same time. In such prayer we

recover our capacity for the "radical amazement" that
Abraham Heschel argued is foundational to a healthy
personality and a sane society.[5]

Nothing and no one were ever admired enough. Adoration is the act in which we freely put ourselves in homage to
that which is more and better than we are—which amounts
to most of what is out there. We are living in a world fecund
in beauty and wild with goodness. We are living with people
who are "the fairest of the sons of men" and "all fragrant
with myrrh and aloes and cassia." Why don't we know it? We
are so preoccupied with the vanities of self-love, daubing
cosmetics on our pinched and emaciated features, that we
are inattentive to the majesty and virility in people and
creatures and God. We are created to adore. When our
instincts operate spontaneously, we adore extravagantly: "My
heart overflows with a goodly theme."

A New Venture in Love

The second half of the psalm, addressed to the queen-bride,
is an admonition to detachment, completing the cure to self-
love.

> *Hear, O daughter, consider, and incline your ear;*
> *forget your people and your father's house;*
> *and the king will desire your beauty.*
> *Since he is your lord, bow to him;*
> *the people of Tyre will sue your favor with gifts,*
> *the richest of the people with all kinds of wealth.*

> *The princess is decked in her chamber with gold-woven robes;*
> *in many-colored robes she is led to the king,*
> *with her virgin companions, her escort, in her train.*
> *With joy and gladness they are led along*
> *as they enter the palace of the king.*

"Hear, O daughter, consider, and incline your ear; forget
your people and your father's house." The Tyrian princess,

brought before the Hebrew king for marriage, is already homesick. She is in a strange country. She is in unfamiliar territory, addressed in strangely accented speech, away from the cozy securities of friends and family. She is full of longings for what she has left. As long as she is attached to her childhood and her family and her customs (that is, the things that certified her acceptance and significance), she is incapable of a new venture in love.

If the first rule of love is astonished recognition ("This at last is bone from my bones, and flesh from my flesh!"—Gen 2:23 JB), the second is that "a man leaves his father and his mother and cleaves to his wife, and they become one flesh" (Gen 2:24). If there is no "leaving," there can be no "cleaving."

Love launches us into new territory. To explore the new, the old must be left. It means leaving earlier levels of accomplishment and relationship and growing into new ones. Every act of love is a risk of the self. There are no guarantees in love. Much can go wrong: we can get hurt; we can be rejected; we can be deceived. But without risking these perils there can only be a repetition of old patterns, the routinization of old comforts.

The self cannot be itself if it does not grow, and for a creature made in the image of God to grow is to love. No living being can be static. The self cannot be preserved in amber. Every new act of love requires detachment from what is outgrown, what serves merely to infantilize us. Karlfried Durckheim used to insist: "You never kill the ego, you only find that it lives in a larger house than you thought." The self, if it is to become itself, must find a larger house to dwell in than the house where everyone coddles us and responds to our whims. The passage from leaving home to entering marriage is the archetypal transition from the comfortable, cared-for self to the strenuous, caring-for self.

Self-love is obsessed with keeping what it has and adding

a little more of the same. That is why it is so boring. There is never anything new to say, nothing new to discover. Self-love assesses its position by what it has and is panicked at the thought of losing any of it. Forced into new relationships, into new situations, its first consideration is not of the new fields for love but of the appalling prospects of loss. So it clings. It holds. And it whines.

The detachment that is prerequisite for mature marriage prepares us for maturity in love across the board. We outlive our past over and over again. There comes a moment when I am no longer a spouse, I am no longer a parent, I am no longer employed, I am no longer healthy. There are periods of my life that are immensely valuable and enjoyable and useful but which by their very nature cannot be perpetuated. Ironically, if we try to perpetuate them in the name of love, we ruin love.

Detachment is not disloyalty; it is a requirement for the next movement of love, which is a movement into a more perfect love. Such movements almost always begin in feelings of loss, of deprivation. But detachment is not loss—it is a precondition for fresh creativity. If we cling to experiences or roles or memories or relationships, we simply become pitiful. Self-love holds on to the good long after it has ceased to be good for us: "forget your people and your father's house." Your father's house was fine when you were a child. There is nothing wrong with it now. But it is no longer large enough for you, if you are to live life to your best. You are now a bride: "the king will desire your beauty." You were beautiful to friends and parents before; now you will be beautiful in a new dimension, beautiful to your husband, your king.

The present situation of the princess is described (vv. 12-15). Is the description a corrective to her self-perceived deprivation? Her gold-woven, many-colored robes, her virgin companions, the parade of joy that is the wedding march—

all this is the actual reality of the present. This is what is going on right now. But in order to be present in this there has to be detachment from the past, leaving the experience of being cherished in order to engage in the experience of cherishing. Nostalgia for the past obscures the splendor of the present.

Why do so many fail to enter the ecstasies of the eternal present? Is it not because of the lazy and sentimental attachments to "Tyre"? Emily Dickinson wrote of "Renunciation—the piercing virtue!"[6] A painful separation from earlier good releases us into the present best. The ascetic denials that are so much a part of the life of faith in no way deny pleasure. They prepare us for it. Marriage is the common-life paradigm for this abandonment of immature treasures that is prerequisite to experiencing the delights of mature intimacies.

Opening Out and Growing Up
The final lines are a promise that comes into fulfillment when the adoration (vv. 1-9) and the detachment (vv. 10-15) are integrated.

Instead of your fathers shall be your sons;
you will make them princes in all the earth.
I will cause your name to be celebrated in all generations;
therefore the peoples will praise you for ever and ever.

Instead of fathers, sons. Instead of a past, a future. Instead of ancestors, descendants. Instead of understanding ourselves by what was given in our inheritance, we understand ourselves by what we become in creating new life.

Self-love is barren, infertile. Love is fertile. Self-love is attached to the familiar, the cozy: possessions, customs. Love is detached from the cloying clutter and therefore open to fertilization by the new, open to the ecstasy of intercourse and the act of creation. Attachment is closed up and walled in. Detachment opens out and grows up.

There is a subtle shift in these lines that goes undetected in English translations, a shift of address from bride to groom (Hebrew distinguishes between the masculine and feminine "your" and "you"). The king-groom is now addressed. He, as well as his bride, must be detached just as he shares the results. Nothing in love is unilateral. Both adoration and detachment require a partner. These things cannot be separated and then assigned to masculine and feminine. Whenever that is done, difference is exploited into subservience. It is one of the oldest tricks of self-love, and it is not permitted. Unself-love embraces the dignities of mutuality and practices the embrace in prayer.

Prayer creates the space that allows us to be detached from what we were convinced was necessary but in fact is only restrictive. We can then be free to receive love, for love can only be experienced as a free act. Prayer creates this detachment from necessity and openness to freedom. Without prayer, in Henri Nouwen's analysis, "our relationships with others easily become needy and greedy, sticky and clinging, dependent and sentimental, exploitative and parasitic. . . . We cannot experience the others as different from ourselves but only as people who can be used for the fulfillment of our own, often hidden, needs."[7]

Worldly wisdom concedes that love is marvelous in the bedroom, but it is convinced that it has no place in government. It expects protestations of love on a beach in the moonlight but finds them embarrassingly out of place around the conference table of a corporate board room. The problem is that nothing in all of biblical literature corroborates that contention. God is not only engaged in loving each person in a saving way, he is bringing a kingdom into being. Moreover, the whole of Scripture tells us that the same God who rules the world saves the soul.

No one has difficulty believing that the central characteristic of God is love, for "God is love" (1 Jn 4:16). The texts are clear that God acts in love, both to individuals and to the public. "Jesus loves me this I know, for the Bible tells me so," if not a scriptural citation is at least an accurate summary of Scripture. But so is "God so loved the world" (Jn 3:16). World and self are the double foci of God's love. God does not have one form of action for the world and another for individuals. God does not deal with the soul on the basis of personal love and with the nation on the basis of impersonal expediency. He does not engage in redemptive love among persons and then take police action in world history. It is love both times.

It is quite true that the expressions of love in society and culture require different forms from those within families and among friends. The usual form in which love comes to expression in the public sector is a passion for justice. Legislation rather than kisses, the vigorous pursuit of policy rather than the carefully timed presentation of a dozen roses, is the means. But what must not change is the biblical base of love. Love—not expediency, not profit motives—is still the base, and that must not be displaced by anything, or any one.

Spontaneity in Love

To prevent such displacement, people of faith pray. Prayer is the form in which love can be exercised in society as in the self. Here too prayer involves adoration and detachment. In generously praising what is there and in firmly refusing to clingingly possess it, mature love is developed. In such prayers, other selves are affirmed and set free. Society is given space to develop in love, neither demoralized by denigration nor clogged with acquisitiveness. The praying of such praised and released selves infiltrates society in ways that free it for spontaneity in love in both its personal and public forms.

Marriage is the normative (but not exclusive) way in which people experience and practice this life of love. This setting requires the integration of the personal and the public. Every marriage brings two unrelated families into committed historical encounter with each other. Every society has taboos against incest and laws against marrying within families. There are genetic, but also political, reasons for this. Ingrownness is bad biologically; it is also bad socially. We need to be forced out of ourselves into encounter with others and to demonstrate with our lives that the other is an ally and not an enemy. Strangers, through the practice of adoration and detachment, become lovers. The natural rivalries that develop between people who are different are countered in the act of marriage and changed into alliances.

This was obvious on an international level when ancient and medieval marriages were arranged between royal houses, as in Psalm 45. But it is no less true in the neighborhood. Every marriage crosses another boundary of genealogy. Disparate histories are brought together in such a way that the other is presented for appreciation and praise, not contempt and rejection. Every marriage is proof that the other is not the enemy, not the rival, not the threat, but the friend, the ally and, at best, the lover.

An Archetypal Act of Freedom
All marriages are ventured into with this possibility and expectation, but they do not all confirm it. Marriages fail. Partners become rivals, jealous and threatened, rejecting and rejected. Betrayals occur. Still, the most significant recurring act of love that takes place in society is marriage. Ezra Pound was radical in his claim for it: "One humane family can humanize a whole state into courtesy; one grasping and perverse man can drive a nation to chaos."[8] Quite regardless of the number of failures, the cumulative effect of the multiplied ventures is positive, countering the ingrownness of the self.

Marriage is an archetypal act of freedom. Marriage partners, by leaving their natural family ties, break out of networks of necessity and predictability and at that moment become prime movers in the politics of freedom. This is true even in an arranged marriage: though the free will of the partners is not consulted, the arrangement is a result of *someone's* choice and not the mere product of biological necessity. Every marriage, then, introduces into society fresh energies of love and freedom that have the power to unself not only the lovers themselves but America itself. The mere introduction of these energies is not enough, however, or we would have become Utopia long since. They need continuing and perfecting. Where can we get that but in Christ? A prayed and praying faithfulness carries us into the long life of love in which and by which the world will not perish.

Notes

Chapter 1: The Unselfing of America

[1] Martin Buber, *Meetings,* edited by Maurice Friedman (LaSalle, Ill.: Open Court Publishing Co., 1973), p. 59.

[2] Alexis de Tocqueville, *Democracy in America,* 2 vols. (New York: Schocken Books, 1974), 2:93.

[3] Alexander Solzhenitsyn, "World Split Apart," *Vital Speeches,* Sept. 1, 1978.

[4] Baron Friedrich von Hügel, *Letters from Baron Friedrich von Hügel to a Niece,* edited by Gwendolyn Greene (London: J. M. Dent and Sons Ltd., 1958), p. 25.

[5] John Calvin, *Commentary on the Book of Psalms,* vol. 1 (Grand Rapids: Eerdmans, 1949), p. xxxvii.

[6] G. K. Chesterton, *The Collected Poems* (New York: Dodd, Mead & Co., 1980) pp. 136-37.

[7] Karl Jaspers, *Man in the Modern Age* (Garden City, N.Y.: Anchor Press/ Doubleday, 1951), p. 77.

[8] Wendell Berry, *A Continuous Harmony* (New York: Harcourt Brace Jovanovich, 1972), p. 79.

[9] "Today, part of the pathology of western Christian life is the destruction of the essential unity of the mystical and the socio-political, the contemplative and the prophetic. Mysticism and politics are seen at best as alternative modes of discipleship, at worst as incompatible and ideological opposites. So we have forms of escapist, pietistical, anticarnational spirituality on the one hand, and forms of fanatical, inhuman, antiincarnational political movements on the other. In both one sees a failure to treat the human seriously." Kenneth Leech, *The Social God* (London: Sheldon Press, 1981), p. 27.

[10]Quoted by Berry, *A Continuous Harmony*, p. 15.

Chapter 2: Unself-Made

[1]Jürgen Moltmann, *The Church in the Power of the Spirit* (New York: Harper & Row, 1975), p. 279.

[2]Mitchell Dahood, *The Psalms*, 3 vols. (Garden City, N.Y.: Doubleday, 1975), 2:298.

[3]Martin Buber, *On the Bible*, edited by Nahum Glatzer (New York: Schocken Books, 1968), pp. 11-12.

[4]"In the Diaspora, conversion was a voluntary act by masses of Gentiles who wished to join the Jewish people of faith." *The Jewish People in the First Century*, 2 vols. edited by S. Safrai and M. Stern (Philadelphia: Fortress Press, 1976), 2:622.

[5]The LXX mistranslated the Hebrew of v. 5, "O Mother Zion." The mistranslation resulted, probably, from a textual error in the Greek, *meter* for *meti*. But the mistranslation catches the spirit of the psalm too strikingly to be dismissed without notice. (James Joyce often retained the mistakes that typists made in transcribing his crabbed handwriting, believing that they had improved on what he had written.)

[6]It is interesting to recall that in the Greek city-states the public realm was regularly viewed as the place of freedom, in contrast to the private realm that was a place of necessities. In private one was hemmed in by the necessities of spouse and children, clothing, food, housing; in the public realm, in politics, there was scope for freely creating patterns of association and responsibility that would enhance life beyond its survival aspects. Jesus deepened that insight immeasurably with his proclamation of the kingdom, God's public realm. It is essential to regain this public ground that has been lost to an aggressive secularism abetted by a privatized pietism. Prayer is the primary means in this work of reclamation. See Elizabeth Young-Bruehl, *Hannah Arendt: For Love of the World* (New Haven: Yale University Press, 1982), p. 319.

[7]Eugene H. Peterson, "Festival" in *A Widening Light*, ed. Luci Shaw (Wheaton, Ill.: Harold Shaw, 1984), p. 119.

Chapter 3: Unself-Centered

[1]Donald Baillie, *God Was in Christ* (London: Faber & Faber Ltd., 1956), pp. 43-44.

[2]Thomas Hardy, *The Complete Poems* (New York: Macmillan, 1982), p. 572.

[3]A. F. Kirkpatrick, *Commentary on the Psalms* (London: Cambridge University Press, 1947), p. 665.

[4]Quoted by Dahood, *The Psalms*, 3:113.

[5]Ezra Pound, *Selected Poems* (New York: New Directions, 1957), p. 82.

[6]A similar picture is reconstructed by modern scholars, but in terms of an ancient enthronement ceremony in which the king is led down to the foot of the hill of Jerusalem to the spring of Gihon. He drinks from the waters of Gihon in a kind of sacramental act and is anointed by the priest. Then, with head lifted high, he proceeds back to the temple area with jubilation and rejoicing, accompanied by shouts of "Long live the king!" (1 Kings 1:32-40). Hans-Joachim Kraus, *Psalmen*, 2nd ed., 2 vols. (Neukirchen Kreis, Moers: Neukirchener Verlag der Buchhandlungdes Erziehungsvereins, 1961), 2:762.

[7]Amitai Etzioni, *An Immodest Agenda* (New York: New Press, 1983).

Chapter 4: Unself-Government

[1]Wendell Berry, *The Unsettling of America* (New York: Avon Books, 1977), p. 55.

[2]Psalms 47, 93, 95—99.

[3]These psalms with their characteristic "the LORD reigns" are a polemic against all pretentions to rule by other gods and kings pretending to be gods. Sigmund Mowinckel, the great Norwegian psalms scholar, has argued that they were sung at a New Year's Day ritual that greeted God in an act of worship as the king who renewed his dominion by recreating the world. "There is in this proclamation a confession against the great monarchies of the East and their religion. Neither Marduk nor Assur, but Yahweh, became king and is now king and will be king when all other powers vanish. *Yahweh malak* has to be translated: Yahweh became king (in the first creation), he becomes king (now in his enthronement on New Year's Day, the day of the world renewed by him), and will become king (at the day of the eschatological 'second' creation)." Johannes Hemple, *Interpreter's Dictionary of the Bible*, 3:949. See also H. H. Rowley, *The Old Testament and Modern Study* (London: Oxford University Press, 1952), pp. 190-92.

[4]This number includes kings of the united kingdom and of both northern and southern kingdoms after the schism.

[5]Acts 8:1, 3; 9:1; matched by 9:1-19; 22:4-16; 26:9-18.

[6]Amos Oz, *My Michael* (New York: Alfred A. Knopf, 1972), p. 115.

[7]As a noun in Song 1:10; as a verb in 1:5; 2:14; 4:3; 6:4.

[8]Herbert Butterfield, *Writings on Christianity and History* (New York: Oxford University Press, 1979), p. 57.

Chapter 5: Unself-Help

[1]Harry Blamires, *Tyranny of Time* (New York: Morehouse-Barlow Co.,

1965), p. 98.

[2]Dahood's translation of v. 3 reads "we will not fear the jaws of the nether world." *The Psalms*, 1:278.

[3]I am oversimplifying. There are many who are in prisons, mental hospitals and armies for nonviolent reasons, and there are honorable, praying Christians in all these places. But prisons, asylums and armies do, nonetheless, represent the conspicuous locations of organized violence in our time.

[4]The refrain is missing after the first stanza in the oldest manuscripts and therefore omitted in many translations. But it is generally assumed that the omission is due to a copyist's error, so I have included it. See Artur Weiser, *The Psalms* (Philadelphia: Westminster, 1962), pp. 368-69.

[5]Charles Norris Cochrane gives a brilliant exposition of Augustine in these matters in *Christianity and Classical Culture* (New York: Oxford University Press, 1957), esp. chap. 12, "Divine Necessity and Human History," pp. 456ff.

[6]Dahood, *The Psalms*, 1:279, 281.

[7]Georges Bernanos, *The Diary of a Country Priest* (Garden City, N.Y.: Image Books/Doubleday, 1954), p. 164.

[8]Dahood on the basis of Ugaritic parallels is convincing, I think, that *desolation* is an antonym of *wars* and therefore to be rendered *fertility*. *The Psalms*, 1:281.

[9]Annie Dillard, *Pilgrim at Tinker Creek* (New York: Harper's Magazine Press, 1974), p. 137.

[10]This is not to say that there are not historical situations in which we are permitted, even commanded, to engage in war. I understand the commanded wars of Israel in this context—the best possible action under the circumstances but not therefore a justification for war as such. The question of the "just war" has taxed the intelligence and conscience of Christians for centuries. In my judgment the question is getting less complex by the day: the potential for nuclear war will soon make pacifists of us all (but not passivists).

[11]Baron Friedrich von Hügel, *Selected Letters 1896-1924*, edited by Bernard Holland (New York: E. P. Dutton & Co., 1933), p. 147.

[12]Miguel de Unamuno, *The Agony of Christianity* (New York: Frederick Ungar Publishing Co., 1960), p. 51.

Chapter 6: Unself-Assertion

[1]William Barrett, *The Illusion of Technique* (Garden City, N.Y.: Anchor Press/Doubleday, 1978), p. 232.

[2]Peter Berger, *Invitation to Sociology* (Garden City, N.Y.: Anchor Press/

Doubleday, 1963), pp. 132-34.

[3]John Henry Newman, *The Idea of a University* (Notre Dame, Ind.: University of Notre Dame Press, 1982), p. 156.

[4]D. H. Lawrence proposed a sartorial remedy: have everyone put on red trousers so that no one would appear bedraggled or inconsequential!

Chapter 7: Unself-Pity

[1]St. Gregory Nazianzus, *Oratio 38*, quoted by Thomas Merton, *Seasons of Celebration* (New York: Farrar, Straus and Giroux, 1978), p. 13.

[2]Harry Stack Sullivan, *The Collected Works of Harry Stack Sullivan*, 2 vols. (New York: W. W. Norton, 1953), 1:202.

[3]Dahood, *The Psalms*, 2:227.

[4]"The World According to Russell Baker," *Johns Hopkins Magazine* 24 (1983):8.

[5]Dillard, *Pilgrim at Tinker Creek*, p. 271.

Chapter 8: Unself-Righteous

[1]C. S. Lewis, *The Problem of Pain* (New York: Macmillan, 1953), p. 141.

[2]Fyodor Dostoevsky, *The Brothers Karamazov* (New York: Heritage Press, 1949), pp. 179-86.

[3]Alasdair MacIntyre, *Against the Self-Images of the Age* (Notre Dame, Ind.: University of Notre Dame Press, 1978), p. 26.

[4]Gerhard van Rad, *Old Testament Theology*, 2 vols. (New York: Harper & Row, 1962), 1:400.

[5]Ronald J. Sider, *Rich Christians in an Age of Hunger* (Downers Grove, Ill.: InterVarsity Press, 1978), p. 85.

[6]Martin Hengel, *Property and Riches in the Early Church* (Philadelphia: Fortress, 1974), p. 45.

[7]The word translated "plans of the poor" can also be translated "company of the poor." *Counsel* is also *council*. See Dahood, *The Psalms*, 1:82.

[8]Charles Williams, *He Came Down from Heaven* (London: Faber & Faber, 1956), p. 63.

[9]Simon Tugwell, *The Beatitudes: Soundings in Christian Tradition* (Springfield, Ill.: Templegate Publishers, 1980), p. 26.

[10]Christopher Lasch has examined this phenomenon from the perspective of sociology. He believes that the cause is not loss of interest in God but in the future and in the past, which gradually erodes community to what is most immediate and finally diminishes it to the immediacy of the self. See *The Culture of Narcissism* (New York: W. W. Norton, 1968), p. 211.

[11]Johannes Pederson, *Israel, Its Life and Culture*, vols. 1-2 (London: Oxford University Press, 1946), pp. 429, 539.

Chapter 9: Unself-Serving

[1]Dorothy L. Sayers, *Creed or Chaos?* (New York: Harcourt, Brace & Co., 1949), pp. 56-57.

[2]Irenaeus, *Against Heresies*, quoted by Kenneth Leech, *The Social God* (London: Sheldon Press, 1981), p. 27.

[3]Athanasius, *On the Incarnation*, quoted by Louis Bouyer, *A History of Christian Spirituality*, vol. 1 (New York: Seabury Press, 1982), p. 418.

[4]Charles Williams, *The Descent of the Dove* (New York: Living Age Books, 1956), p. 51.

[5]Leech, *The Social God*, p. 34.

[6]"In every single point we have apparent clearness while all is hollow and formal, a boyish enthusiasm for playing with husks and shells, and a childish satisfaction in the working out of empty syllogisms." Adolf Harnack, *History of Dogma*, 7 vols. (New York: Dover Publications, 1961), 4:41-42. Cochrane, in his cogent analysis of the controversy, wrote: "Arianism has been described as a common-sense heresy, and it has been suggested that the real trouble with the heresiarch was that 'he could not understand a metaphor.' " *Christianity and Classical Culture*, p. 233.

[7]Charles Péguy, *Basic Verities* (New York: Pantheon Books, 1943), p. 109.

[8]The usual interpretation is that the vision depicts pagan dieties assembled before a heavenly tribunal, where God passes judgment on them because their moral obtuseness is responsible for disorders, both cosmic and social. See Dahood, *The Psalms*, 2:268. I have no objection to the possibility that the imagery of the vision comes from some such mythology, but in its *canonical* context, the psalm seems to me far more likely to have been prayed out of the material of actual personal and historical experience.

[9]Gregory of Nyssa, *From Glory to Glory* (New York: Charles Scribner's Sons, 1961), p. 190.

[10]I owe this reference to Annie Dillard, *Living by Fiction* (New York: Harper & Row, 1982), p. 173.

Chapter 10: Unself-Sufficient

[1]Austin Farrer, *Finite and Infinite* (Westminster: Dacre Press, 1959), p. 94.

[2]Ian L. McHarg, *Design with Nature* (Garden City, N.Y.: The Natural History Press, 1969).

[3]Quoted by Barrett, *The Illusion of Technique*, p. 335.

[4]An excellent presentation of both the history of attitudes and the current situation is in *Earthkeeping*, edited by Loren Wilkinson (Grand Rapids: Eerdmans, 1980), p. 19.

[5]A clear accounting of the uniqueness of Israel's faith-life in relation to its religious environment is in G. E. Wright, *The Old Testament against Its Environment* (Chicago: Alec Allenson, Inc., 1955).

[6]Berry, *A Continuous Harmony*, p. 12.

[7]Barrett, *The Illusion of Technique*, p. 173.

Chapter 11: Unself-Love

[1]Anthony Bloom, *Beginning to Pray* (New York: Paulist Press, 1970), p. xiv.

[2]Berry, *A Continuous Harmony*, p. 80.

[3]Henri Troyat, *Tolstoy* (Garden City, N.Y.: Doubleday, 1967), p. 439.

[4]Lasch, *The Culture of Narcissism*, pp. 72-73.

[5]Abraham Joshua Heschel, *God in Search of Man* (New York: Farrar, Straus and Giroux, 1955), p. 46.

[6]Emily Dickinson, *The Complete Poems* (Boston: Little, Brown & Co., 1960).

[7]Henri Nouwen, *Reaching Out* (Garden City, N.Y.: Doubleday, 1975), p. 30.

[8]Quoted by Berry, *A Continuous Harmony*, p. 41.